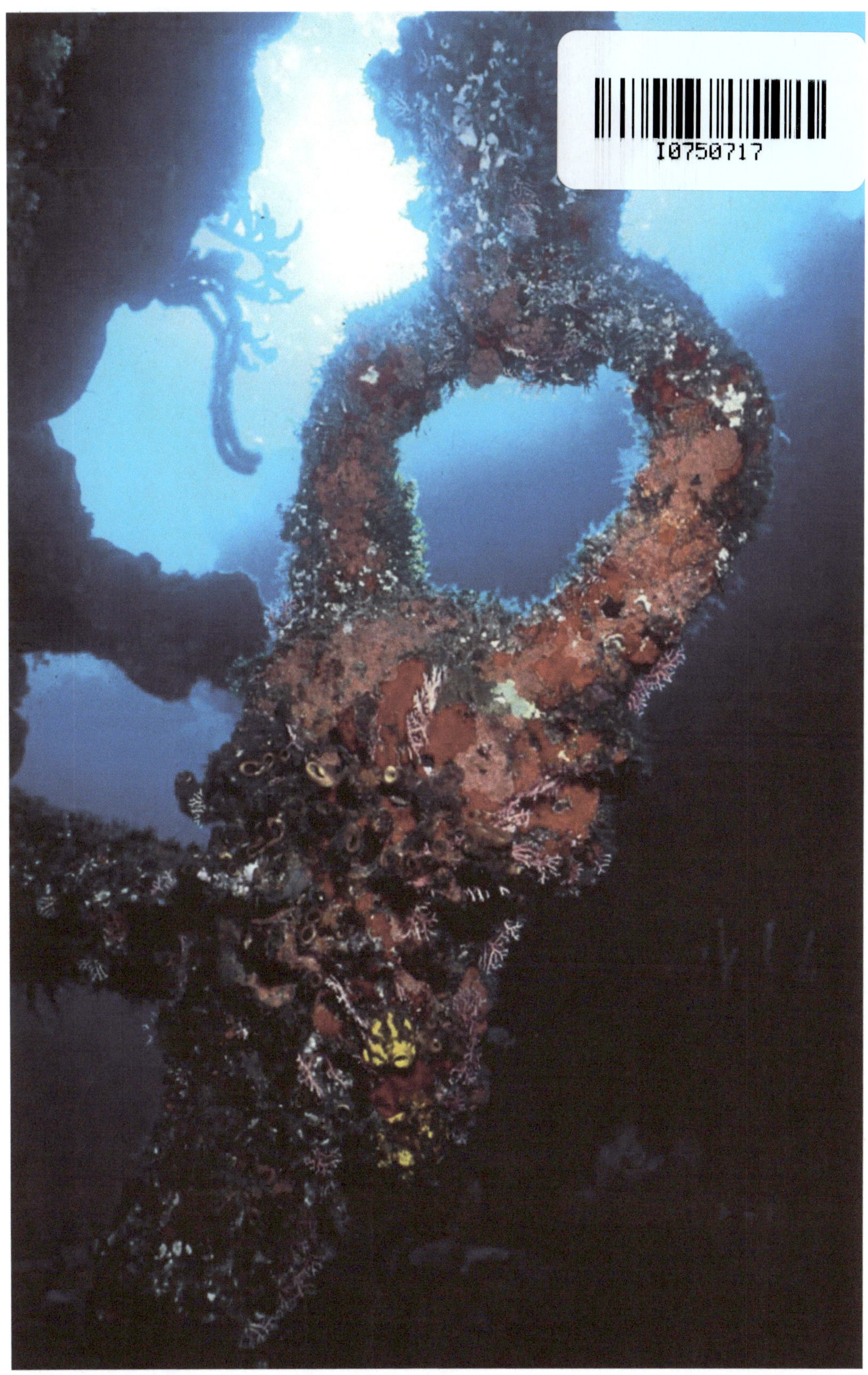

Published by:
Heinerth Productions Inc.
5989 NE County Road 340
High Springs, Fl 32643 USA

First published 2010

All photography and text by Jill Heinerth



This manual is not intended to be used as a substitute for proper dive training. Diving is a dangerous sport and training should only be conducted under the safe supervision of an active diving instructor until you are fully qualified, and then, only in conditions and circumstances which are as good or better than the conditions in which you were trained. Careful risk assessment, continuing education and skill practice may lessen your likelihood of an accident, but are never a guarantee for complete safety.

This book assumes a basic knowledge of diving technique and should be used to complement a training course specializing in underwater photography techniques.

Cover Photo: The author snaps a self portrait as she descends into her local cave, Ginnie Springs. At times, the tannic water from the Santa Fe River mixes with the turquoise spring water creating unusual color effects.

Book design by Heinerth Productions Inc.
www.IntoThePlanet.com

Printed in the USA

ISBN 978-0-9798789-2-3

## About the Author

Jill Heinerth is an explorer. For over twenty years, her curiosity and photographic skills have given us a tantalizing peek at a breathtaking underwater world few will ever experience.

Best known as a pioneering technical diver, Jill combines a mastery of underwater technology with a formal Fine Arts education to produce artistic documentation of the natural environment above, below and inside our planet.

An award-winning filmmaker, Jill co-wrote, produced, and appeared in *Water's Journey,* the PBS documentary series that takes viewers on visceral travels through the world's greatest water systems. Hollywood directors call on her to produce difficult underwater scenes and international magazines and websites look to her to document extreme environments with high technology.

Jill is a reasonable voice in the world of conservation, and is often sought out for insightful commentary by the media, government, and academic institutions.

Jill's many diving accomplishments are highlighted by an Antarctic cave diving expedition inside B-15, the largest iceberg known to man, (National Geographic - *Ice Island*), and significant contributions to the United States Deep Caving Team's, *Wakulla* 2 project, which used paradigm-changing technology to map an underwater cave system in three dimensions. At Wakulla, secondary to a scientific mission, Jill established a women's diving world record.

Some of Jill's numerous professional diving, photographic and filmmaking awards include: *Sport Diving* Magazine: Named A Living Legend, Women Diver's Hall of Fame: Inaugural Inductee, Explorer's Club Film Festival: Best Documentary, Canadian Technical Diver of the Year, Fellow: National Speleological Society as well as top honors from the International HD Film Fest, Cine Golden Eagle, and Aurora Awards. Jill was also honored by Keen Footwear as a top environmental photographer, bringing attention to the crisis of diminishing freshwater resources.

Jill Heinerth holds various scuba, cave diving, and closed circuit rebreather instructor credentials. An *Adobe Photoshop* expert, she also teaches specialized underwater digital photography workshops and classes. With a wealth of experience as a former owner of a Toronto ad agency, Jill accepts select advertising clients, applying her distinct skill set to each application.

Jill gives upbeat, entertaining, and informative multimedia presentations to groups, clubs and organizations on a wide range of subjects including exploration, motivation and actualization, conservation, risk management, and filmmaking.

Born in Canada, Jill lives with her husband, Robert, in North Florida, where she starts most days with a refreshing swim in the clear water of her local spring.

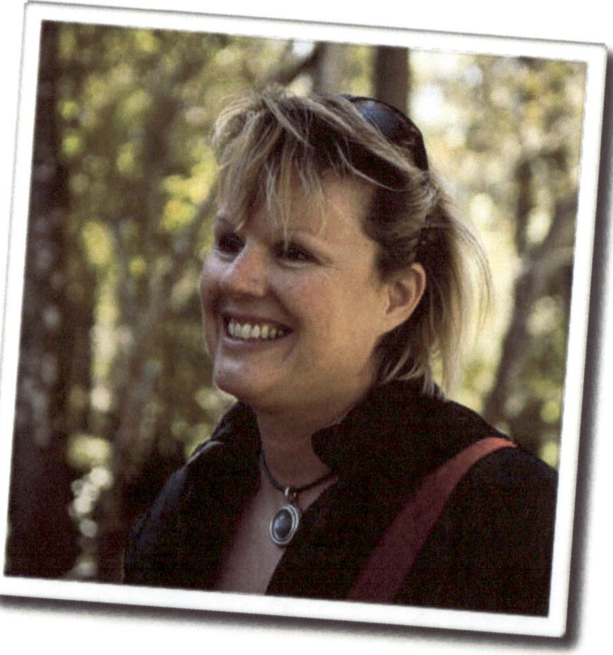

## About the Editor

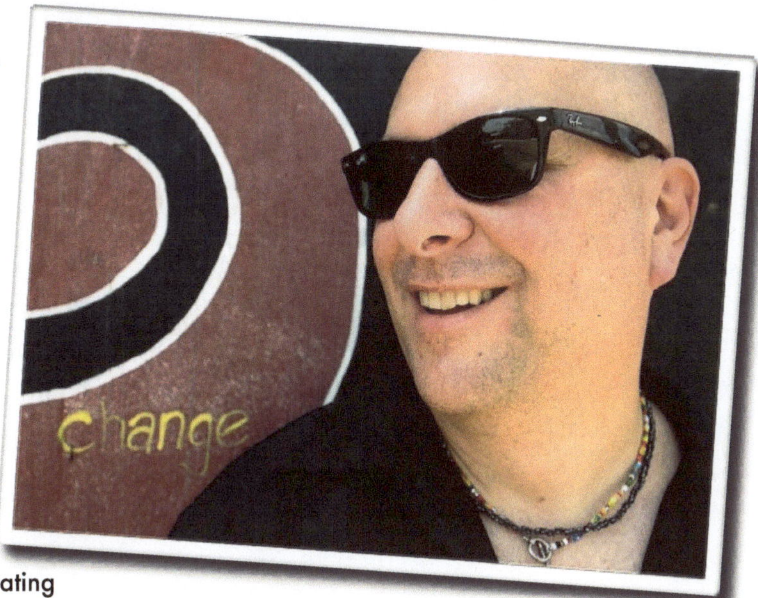


First picking up a 35mm SLR camera at the age of fourteen, Robert McClellan discovered his unique observation skills while documenting the visual world around him. As a young man, he approached a Navy recruiter and agreed to join on one condition: that he could become a combat photographer. After successfully earning the "PH" rating at the prestigious U.S. Naval Schools of Photography, at NAS, Pensacola, Florida, Robert was assigned to the famed Navy SeaBees. Telling the 'Bees story afforded him many opportunities to travel the world, discover colorful cultures, and, along the way, collect two Thomas Jefferson awards for military publishing and photography. Returning to Pensacola as an instructor, Robert trained a future generation of Navy and Marine Corps photographers.

Robert produced and appeared in the award-winning documentary film *Real Sobriety*. He is a new media expert, blogging, podcasting, and keeping abreast of the latest social media trends for his clients. Following on the heels of a stint in radio broadcasting, he now uses his voice talent for commercial clients in advertising, e-books and online instructional manuals.

Living in north Florida provides Robert many opportunities to dive in the fabulous springs and rivers near his home. Lucky for him, his wife (and dive instructor) is patient, and doesn't seem to mind tagging along on his casual open water forays. Although he once owned one, he will probably never dive a rebreather.

## Want to Learn More?

Jill Heinerth and Robert McClellan offer specialized training opportunities for individuals and groups. Contact them through their website at: www.IntoThePlanet.com.

To Cori Rabjohn and Rae McClellan
and all the other young photographers who
strive to share their creative images of the world.

Shoot. Blog. Share. Dream.
Produce more than you consume on this earth.

# Table of Contents

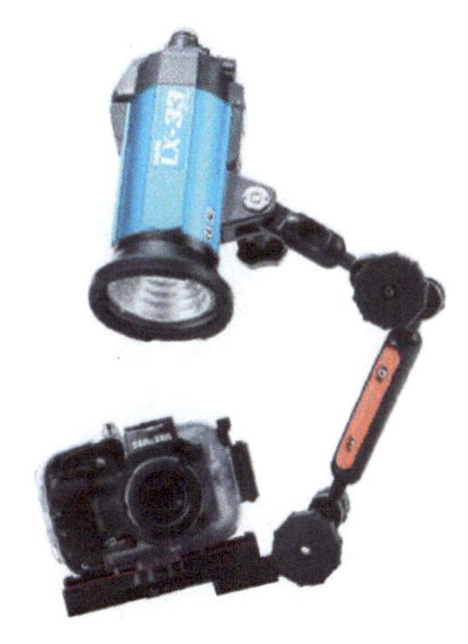

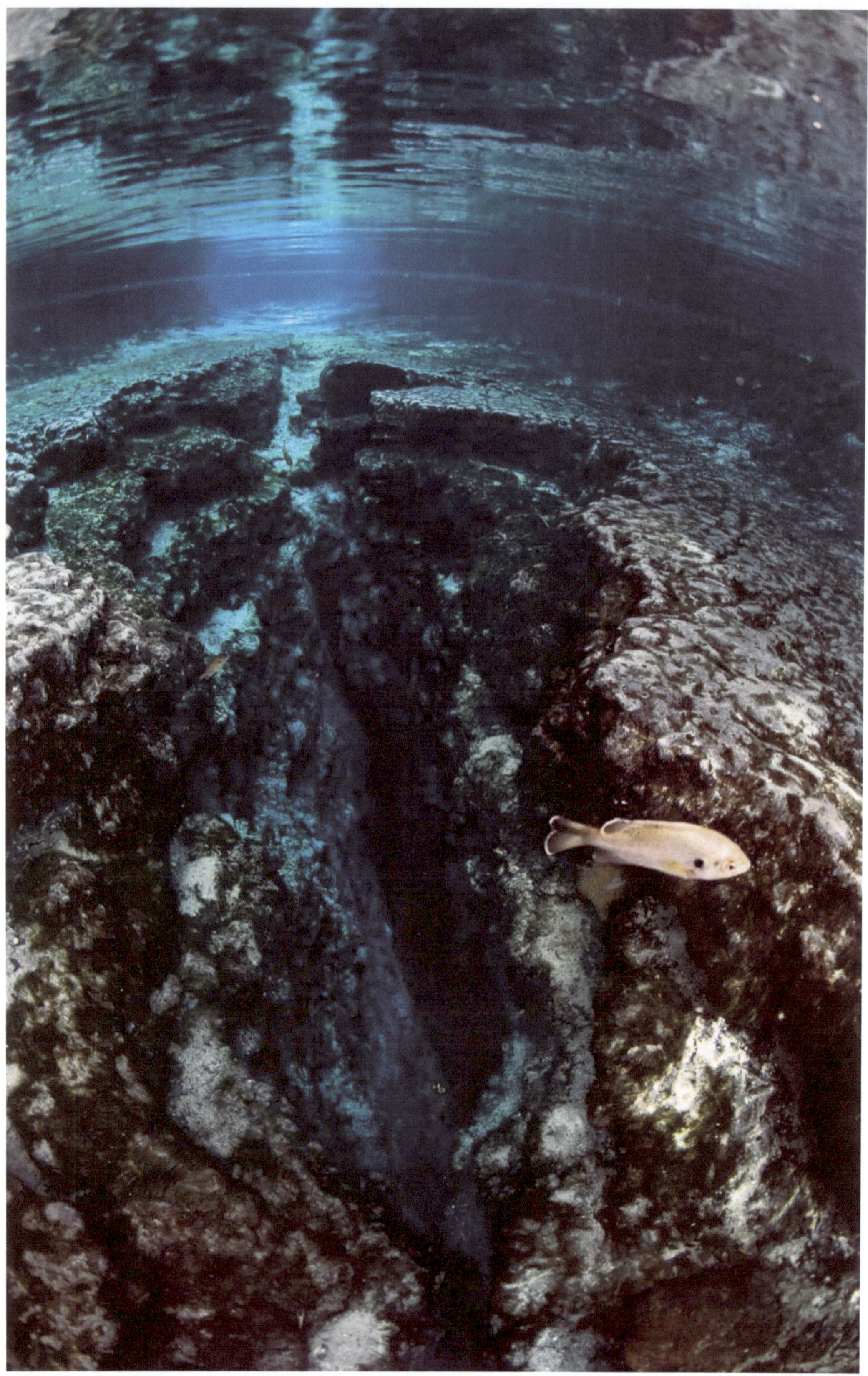

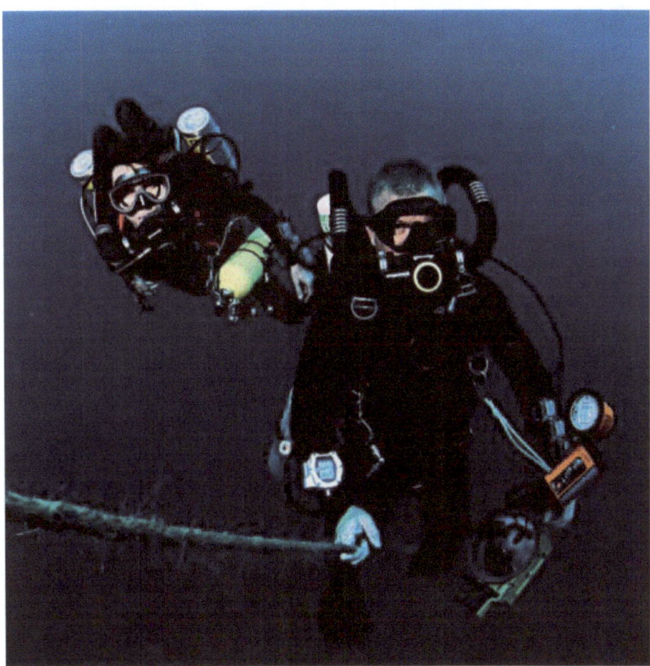

# the basics

## Section One



## Motivation

Whether you are a new diver or an experienced professional, it is appealing to capture the memories of your diving adventures. The *Digital Underwater Photography* manual serves as an introduction to getting the most out of your underwater photography opportunities. Whether you are snorkeling in the crystal clear shallows of a freshwater lake, or diving on deep ocean walls, this guide will help you understand the capabilities of your camera and improve your ability to bring back quality photographs to share with your family, friends and dive buddies.

Underwater photography combines creativity with adventure and gives the diver boundless prospects for recording subjects that few people have ever seen. Underwater photography enhances travel opportunities, adds fun and exciting challenges to your diving excursions and gives you an interesting new pastime to share with your buddy. However, adding a task-load to your recreational diving activities, requires that you sharpen your buoyancy and general diving skills to protect yourself and the environment. This manual will assist you in improving your awareness and technical diving skills as well as your general knowledge of photography and composition for both topside and underwater photographic activities.

## A New Direction

I was a die-hard film shooter, that thought that the purity of emulsion and the magic of the developing tank were the highest forms of art. However, an unfortunate loss at the completion of shooting the Hollywood film, *The Cave*, launched me into the world of digital photography. While we celebrated the show's wrap on a secluded beach in Akumal, Mexico, the security guard from my condo was looting my room of all my cash and photography gear. Although I was living in an overstuffed, travel trailer at the time, I scraped together the needed funds to move into digital photography. Ironically, I had been teaching *Photoshop* editing techniques for well over a decade, but had continued to accept that scanning a slide was somehow more pure than creating a digital file in the first place.

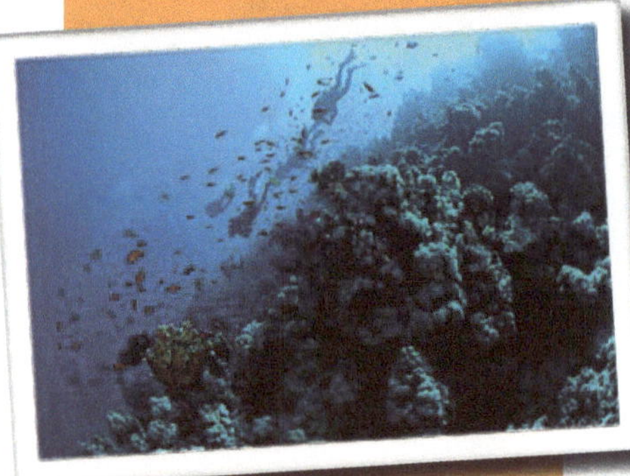

For those that feel that digital photography is somehow a "cheat," think again. The most successful digital photographers have a technical understanding of the limits of their camera system. They also possess a creative understanding of the elements of design and how to unleash the magic through editing. Everything else comes down to practice, persistence, experimentation, and the willingness to go to places that are fresh and new.

# Scope

The *Digital Underwater Photography* manual includes the fundamentals for underwater photography. It provides the basics for using simple and inexpensive underwater cameras and serves as a foundation for divers who are interested in pursuing advanced photography with more complex systems. The book is filled with anecdotes from my personal journey through the world of photography. Filled with expedition tales and first person accounts, I hope you'll find this guide to be your virtual mentor.

# Digital History

In the late 1980s, photographic equipment manufacturer Canon, created a company division called "Still Video." They introduced some of the first digital cameras in the industry. When these cameras were released to professional news photographers, many people debated whether they would be accepted by traditional media outlets. Concerns about overzealous editors manipulating images led to serious concern about whether newspapers and magazines would ever accept a digitally produced photo as authentic. However, the ease of capturing and editing digital images, soon convinced industry skeptics that digital photography was here to stay. Before long, companies like Apple, Nikon, Kodak, and Sony offered consumer-level digital cameras to an eager public. Their ease of use, improved optics and instant visual gratification, accelerated their acceptance among hobbyists and professionals alike.

Digital cameras closely resemble their precursor, film cameras. The biggest difference between a film camera and a digital camera is how the photograph is stored. A digital camera stores photos on a media card that can be bought in various sizes. Media cards offer considerably more storage than conventional rolls of 35 mm film, which usually limited shooters to no more than 36 frames before changing film. A digital photographer can take up to hundreds of shots and edit them on the fly, discarding and overwriting lesser quality images. This has tremendous advantages for photographers working underwater in extreme environments. Prior to the current technology, frequent film changes meant ending the dive to reload in a dry environment.

## Dive Team Roles

To give an underwater scene a sense of scale, it is usually best to use a dive buddy as a model. People who have not experienced a reef, wreck or cave, have no idea how vast the environment is unless you give them something familiar with which to interpret scale. Your model can double as your safety diver, with skills to protect the environment and execute a safe and successful shoot.

When models are used for complex lighting scenarios, they will be holding and directing strobes. For best results, it is important that they understand the creative vision and composition you have in mind for a shot. Simple signals for strobe direction and posing are important to communicate before leaving the surface.

### The Mavica

In 1999, I had the unique opportunity to use a Sony Mavica camera during the filming of National Geographic's, *Mapping the Labyrinth*. The camera was hard mounted to my scooter on a rotating base, allowing me to film myself or the cave as I traveled. Conceived in 1981, the Mavica was the first camera to use a removable disk for recording. The sensor in the camera produced a video signal in a reasonable enough resolution for television. This package was a bit of a hydrodynamic drag, but survived the rigors of five hours at 300 feet, followed by a very lengthy decompression.

## Communication

There are several important visual signals that will help a model understand the photographer's intent for a particular shot. They are illustrated below:

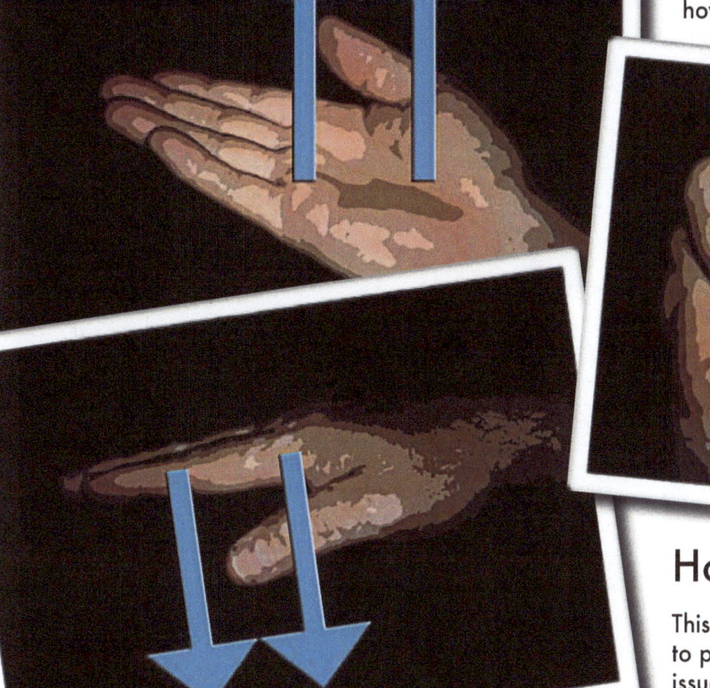

## Move Up / Down

Use these signals to ask your model to move slightly higher or lower in the water column. The size of the gesture lets them know how much to move up or down.

## Hold

This command asks team members to pause while you work on an issue. It is also used to indicate to a model that they have achieved the correct position for the shot.

## Come Here

Use this signal to ask your model to move towards the camera.

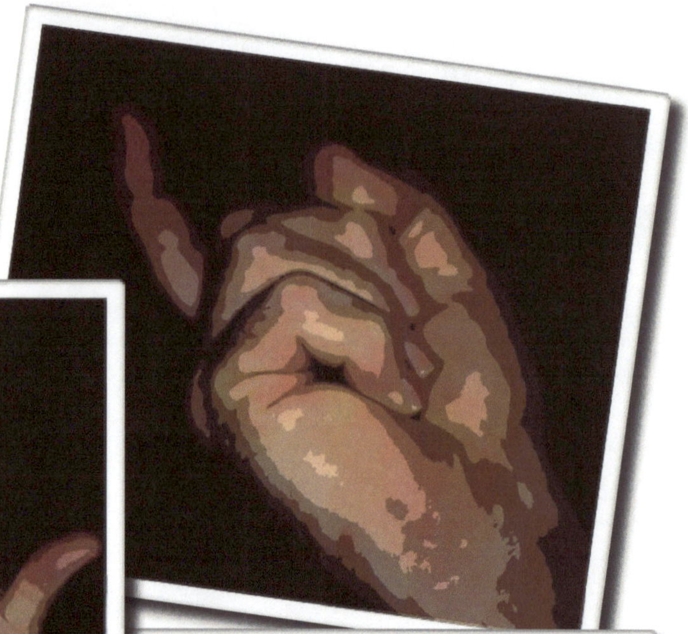

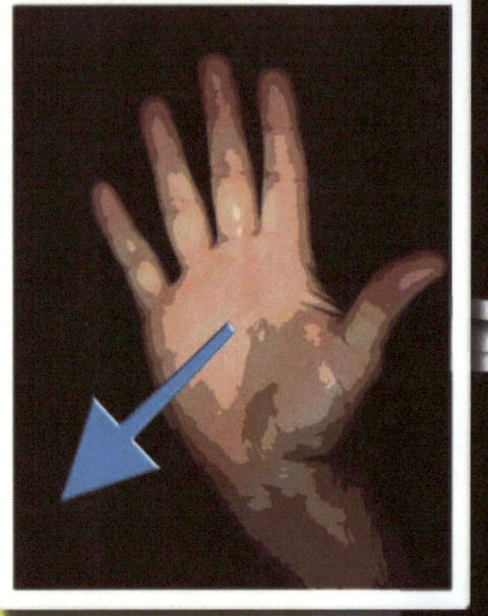

## Move Back

This signal asks the model to back up slightly.

## Question

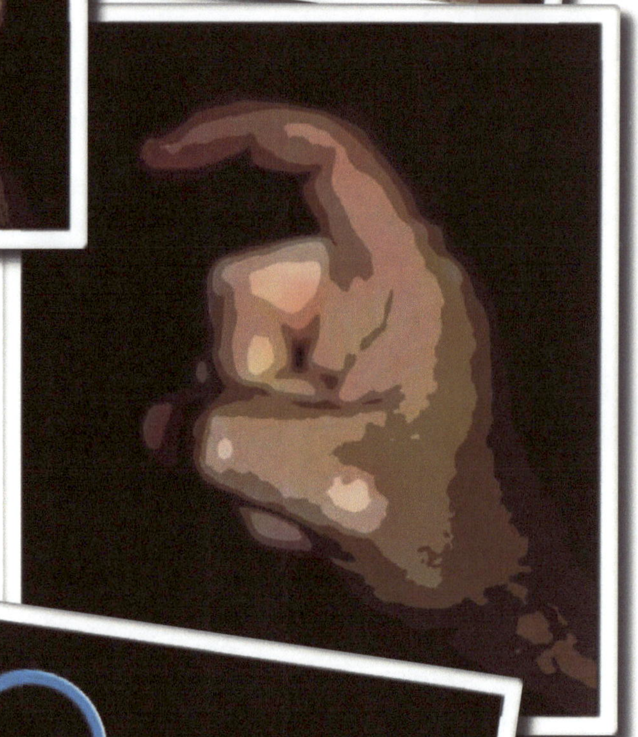

This signal can be used to ask a question like "are your ears okay?" or it may be used by the model if they don't understand the direction from the photographer. It can also be used to indicate "where," as in "where is the boat?"

## Do It Again

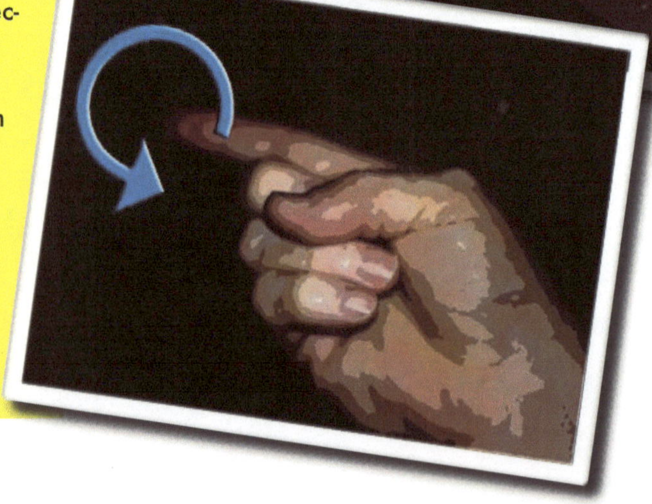

Use this signal to ask the model to repeat the action again.

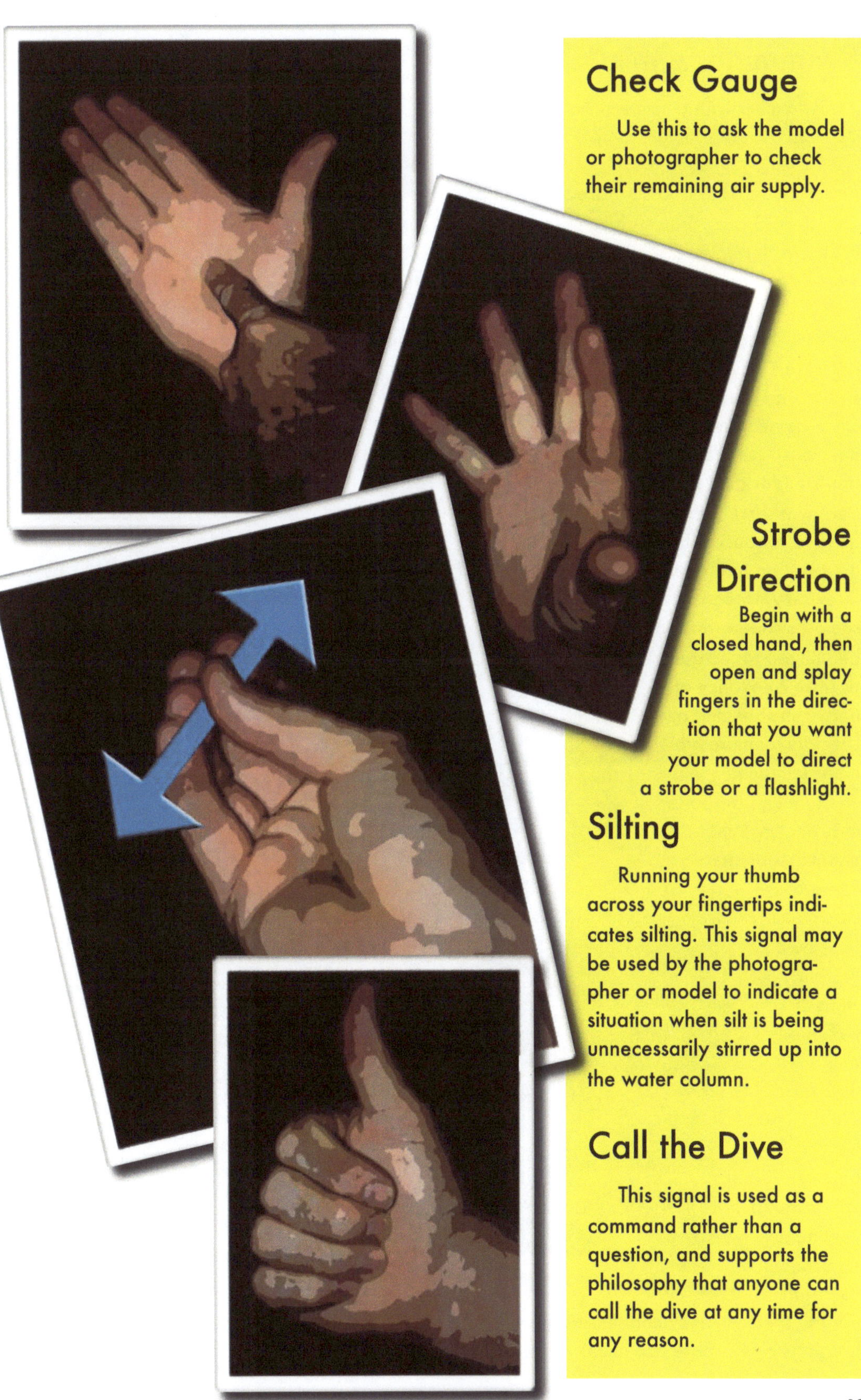

## Check Gauge

Use this to ask the model or photographer to check their remaining air supply.

## Strobe Direction

Begin with a closed hand, then open and splay fingers in the direction that you want your model to direct a strobe or a flashlight.

## Silting

Running your thumb across your fingertips indicates silting. This signal may be used by the photographer or model to indicate a situation when silt is being unnecessarily stirred up into the water column.

## Call the Dive

This signal is used as a command rather than a question, and supports the philosophy that anyone can call the dive at any time for any reason.

## Swimming with a Camera

Swimming with a camera system can be very challenging. Small compact cameras can be easily stashed in a BCD pocket, but larger cameras may create drag as well as a change in body trim. A large camera system with attached strobes will reduce swim speed and range and will usually occupy both hands. It is advisable to trim your photography equipment to as close to neutral as possible. Excessively buoyant systems can be as troublesome as negatively buoyant packages. Very small trim weights (like stainless steel washers) can be affixed to a housing to trim the position and adjust buoyancy. Hollow, sealed strobe arms may be utilized to increase positive buoyancy of heavy strobes and a special incompressible material called syntactic foam can be added to a package that is unnecessarily heavy. Some divers make their own custom, sealed PVC tubes to lighten their load. Air cells are not suitable, because they require continual adjustment as depth varies. The buoyancy characteristics of housings and strobes are usually noted in their technical specifications and should be reviewed before purchase.

Beyond the buoyancy of the package itself, a camera system may alter your personal trim in the water. Holding a slightly negative housing in front of your body will tip your center of gravity to a more head-down position. A positively buoyant housing will pull your upper body higher and, in the case of cave or wreck dives, may cause you to create more silt with your fins. Prior to taking a single picture, it is recommended that divers assemble their camera package and swim with it for a dive or two. Determining how it may affect trim and speed, before adding photographic goals, is time well spent. Your dive buddy can assist you with constructive comments about your streamlining and trim.

## Safety

Underwater photography is a task-loaded activity that will add significant challenges to your diving. Whether you are the model or the photographer, you will learn to refine your buoyancy to a high level of proficiency. You will also find photo dives to be more physically and mentally tiring than most. As a creative endeavor, photography uses the part of your brain that is not very good at keeping track of time and numbers. You will need to remain vigilant about watching your air

supply and depth. Some photographers set their dive watch to beep every five minutes to remind them to check their consumables. Dive buddies and models should be advised to be more active observers of a task loaded photographer.

Some divers choose to attach their camera systems to their body to prevent accidental loss. However, lanyards and other clips can create an unnecessary danger. If there is a need to drop a weight belt, it may become entangled in a lanyard system. For this reason alone, you should always be prepared and able to ditch your camera system in an emergency. It may be an expensive loss, but surely not worth your life. If you cannot consider your camera to be ditchable, then you may want to reconsider your motivations for pursuing underwater photography.

**Section Tip:**
The true artist will learn to look at light. Spend a dive examining how different things look when they are backlit or forelit. Do you like the stark contrast of a backlit seafan shot without strobes? Or do you prefer a well-lit tableau of a colorful fan?

## A Flood of Troubles

In the early nineties, I made some serious life changes. Disenchanted by my partners, I decided to sell my portion of the Toronto advertising business and head to the Cayman Islands. I loved the creative aspects of my career, but needed to find a way to weave that with my love for diving. I landed at a small resort on the secluded East End of Grand Cayman. At the twelve room resort, I would be responsible for diving, marketing and anything from cooking meals to painting walls. It was a time of great freedom. I sold the business, left my boyfriend, had a yard sale and moved south with little more than a suitcase of bikinis and shorts. Knowing that my business partners would be slowly paying me back on a twenty year note, gave me the comfort of having a nest-egg to return to when needed.

On a sunny day close to Christmas, I got a disturbing phone call. A colleague in Toronto gave me the bad news that my former partners had literally closed the business one night and re-opened the following morning under a new name, using all the equipment for chattel on loans. They had decided to evade their debt to me and move on without financial constraint. My nest egg was gone. Thankfully, it was my day off, and I decided that the best way to process the news was to go do what I loved most. I headed out on the morning dive boat and dropped down the wall with my camera. At 165 feet, I felt a tremendous concussion and looked down to see my Nikonos V with 15 mm lens rapidly spewing bubbles. With a decompression obligation hanging over my head, there was nothing to do but watch the salty water seep into the camera body. The system was destroyed.

But at times like these, we often get the greatest clarity. Did I want to return to Toronto and begin a multi-year litigation of revenge against my former partners? With nothing more than a few clothes and a stray dog named Spot, was this the direction I wanted my life to take?

But whether it is a real stripping down to the basics or a metaphoric one, this is how we choose our best course in life. With nothing else to distract me from my goals, I knew that I wanted to be an underwater photographer, no matter the cost.

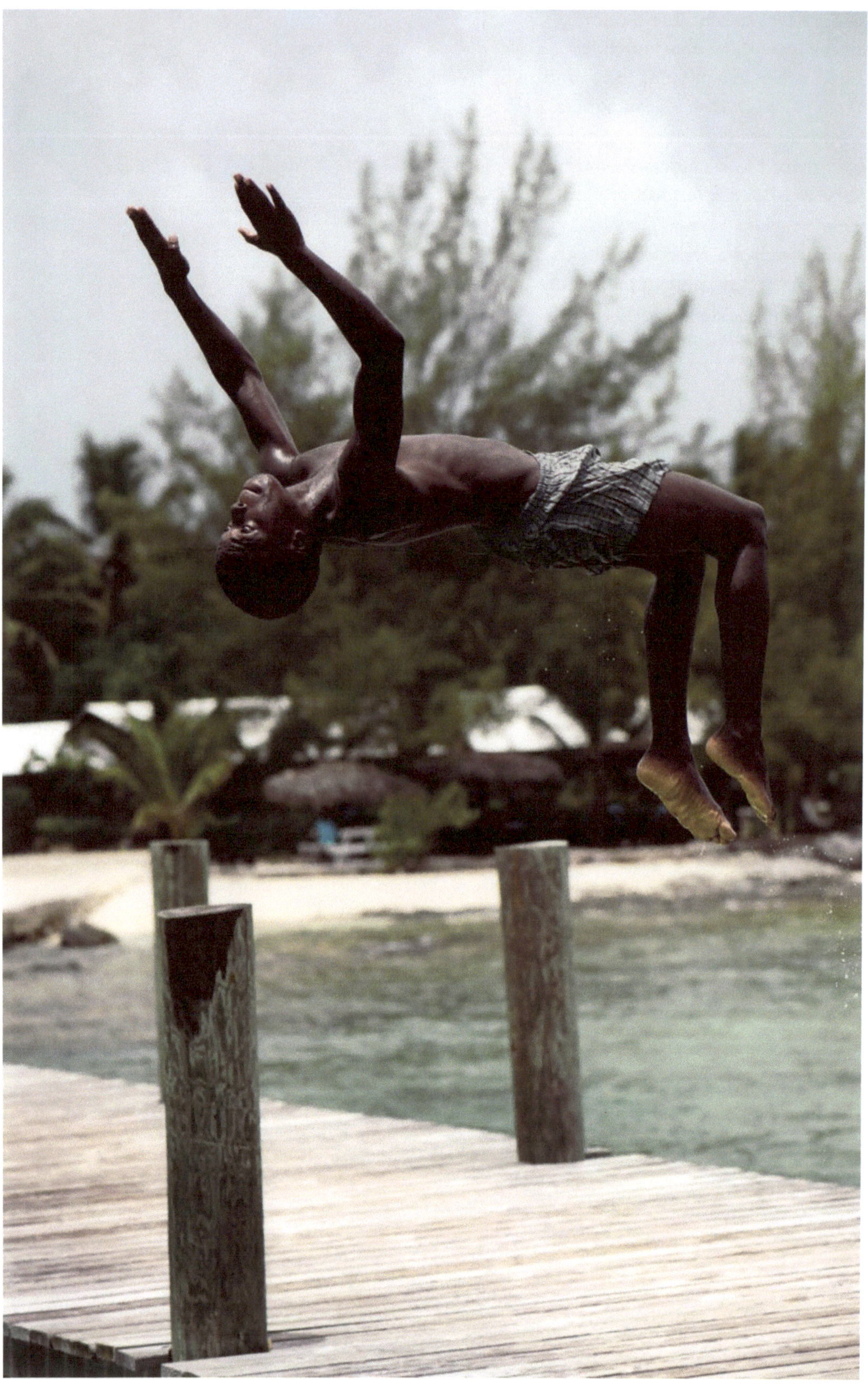

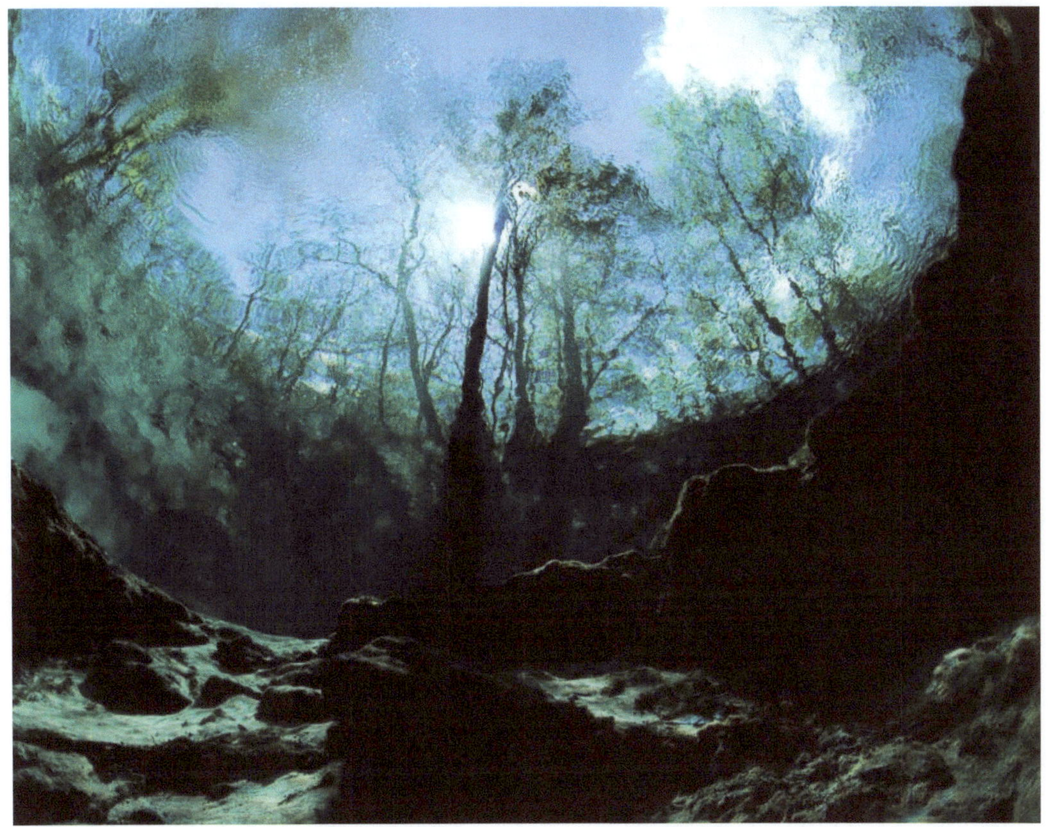

Although this guide book focuses on underwater photography, it is important to remember to shoot both topside and submerged in order to give viewers the full experience of your expedition or trip.

The photo on the facing page is a good example of how a fast shutter speed is used to stop action and freeze the drops of water coming off of the young jumper.

The photo above shows the topside world from the diver's viewpoint. Creative viewpoints give your audience the opportunity to experience a unique perspective on your underwater experiences.

environment

## Section Two



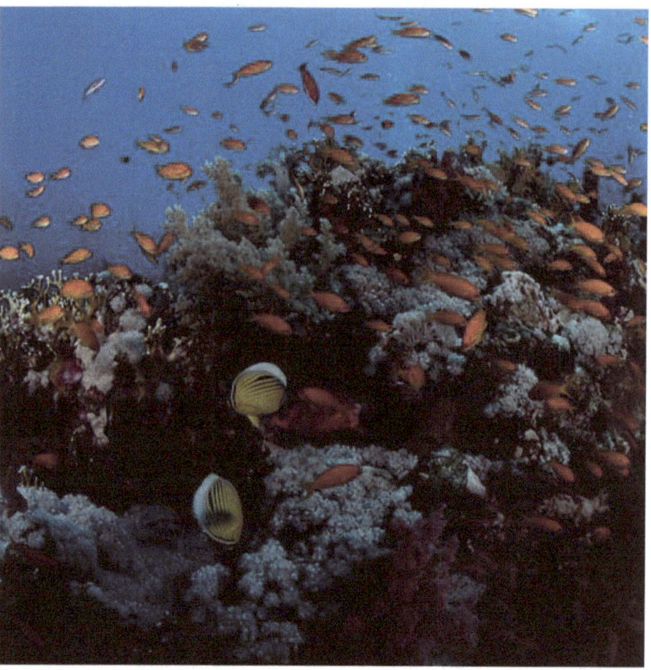

## Temperature

There are several aspects of temperature that may influence your diving. Low surface and water temperatures may present physical diving challenges, and have an impact on your camera and batteries.

In cold water, many divers wear heavy neoprene gloves, mitts, or dry suit gloves. These gloves, though adequate for physical comfort, may limit your ability to manipulate small buttons on camera housings. In some cases, buttons may be impossible to activate with a gloved finger. Many camera controls may be preset before immersion to reduce the need to depress buttons. If you will need to access hard-to-reach controls, you can carry a pencil or similar tool that will allow you to depress the correct button without inadvertently pushing another.

Cold surface and water temperatures may also affect your camera and housing. In the greatest extremes of temperature, the cold may actually shrink critical O-rings and cause leakage into a housing. Careful pre-dive bubble checks are critical. Turn the camera housing to the "on" position to enable the operation of the moisture sensor (if you have this feature). Slowly submerge the housing and watch for leaks. Attach it to a hang line rather than removing it from the water. This helps prevent the camera and housing from freezing in the cold surface air.

Before you hit the water, there are some other precautions to consider. When a camera and housing are stored at two different temperatures or are not allowed to acclimatize, condensation may occur inside the housing, camera and lens. This results in clouding of the photo and potential damage to the camera. It is best to acclimatize both the camera and housing to the local environment. After a period of acclimatization, you can load the housing, knowing it is adjusted to the local temperature and humidity. In other words, when you are in the tropics, you cannot put an air conditioned camera into a warm housing without problems. Even for topside photography, an air-conditioned camera will immediately fog when taken out into a humid, tropical environment.

Some divers place small desiccant packages inside their housing to further reduce condensation issues. These should be replaced on a regular schedule and inspected for breakage. When the soft fabric case breaks, the desiccant crystals can make a big mess inside a housing.

In extremely cold environments, photographers will discover that their camera batteries have a significantly shorter lifespan. Keeping the batteries warm in between dives will increase their life. Chemical or battery operated hand warmers are extremely useful in these environments.

## Visibility

Good visibility will significantly increase your chances of getting great shots, but poor conditions still offer many opportunities. When the water is murky, macro photography is a good choice, since the camera will be placed very close to the subject. Similarly, a wide angle lens allows the diver to get closer to the subject and thus reduce the amount of filtering water between the subject and the lens.

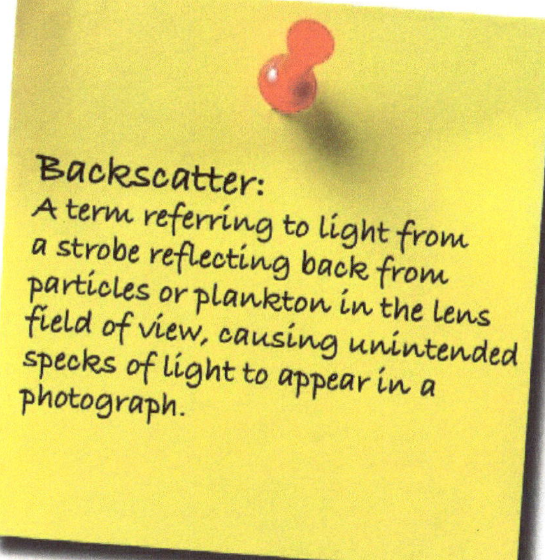


Some water conditions contain a great deal of tiny, solid particles, known as particulate, and the strobe's light reflected from these specks into the lens, creates an undesirable situation known as "backscatter." Strobes mounted on arms allow the photographer to angle the light towards the subject and reduce backscattering. Shooting in shallow water with bright natural light may permit the photographer to use a filter instead of a strobe, thus completely preventing backscatter.

For overall color corrections, pink filters can help in green water, and red filters are used in blue water conditions.

Editing software also presents opportunities for a photographer to improve their image. Most modern photo editing programs contain tools that can manipulate an underwater image to achieve acceptable results. Mastery of post production and editing software is beyond the scope of this book, but will be addressed in advanced editions.

Simple cameras with built in, front-facing flash units will have poor results in turbid water since the front-angled flash unit will cause tremendous backscatter.

## Fish Tales

Stuart Cove's resort in the Bahamas is a photographer's dream. I was participating in an Oceanic Underwater Development Team event, taking the opportunity to capture some shark-feeding behavior. Traveling light, with only a camera and a few clothes, I knew that Oceanic would equip me with their latest kit.

In order to bring out the best of an already artificial environment, we stuffed slabs of raw fish in the pockets of the borrowed gear, knowing this would invoke a riot of fish to follow us around.

I was carefully coached to park myself on the seafloor while the Divemaster positioned himself with a milk crate of bloody fish. Piece by piece, he dispensed the bait on a long pole, satisfying the hungry Leviathans. An agitated woman beside me was attracting a lot of attention from ravenous Yellow Jacks that relentlessly assaulted the mole on her left ear lobe. She pointed anxiously at her hemorrhaging beauty mark, but her husband continued to signal to equalize, assuming that she was having trouble clearing her ears. I flew through a roll of film, knowing that although her marriage might not survive, she would certainly get through the ordeal of fish bites.

At the end of the week, we all purchased the demo gear at a nice discount. Arriving home to my busy life, the dive bag sat percolating on the back porch for several warm days. Only after a flock of menacing vultures began showing interest, did I realize that I had not only imported new dive gear, but also the rotten bait left in the pockets. I was never able to rid the BCDs of the fishy stench and used them instead for attracting predatory attention on future photo dives.

# Water Movement

Currents, tides and surge will all affect the diver's ability to position themselves for a photograph without damaging the environment. Practice hovering in moving water and get used to drifting with the current, without getting too close to corals and other marine life.

High, slack tide tends to offer the best shooting conditions for visibility. Low tide may bring shore particulate into the water, where high tide brings deeper, cleaner ocean water towards shore.

# Fresh versus Saltwater

Excellent subjects are available in both fresh and saltwater environments. Housed cameras allow the photographer to shoot on the boat, half submerged or catch an action shot of divers entering the water.

The main difference between shooting in fresh or saltwater will be the buoyancy of the camera. The diver may need to add small trim weights for salt water. Even a very small stainless washer may be enough to trim the relative position of the camera in the water.

Camera care is even more important in saltwater, since even a small flood in saltwater will usually result in complete loss of the camera.

In between dives, it is best to keep the camera submerged in a tub of freshwater so that salt crystals do not dry on the buttons or lens port. If you don't have a rinse tank available, consider bringing a large Tupperware tub or Pelican case. If the boat is small, then simply wrap the camera in a damp towel.

Take great care when sharing a rinse tub with other photographers. It is in these shared tubs that most lens port scratches occur. It is also the place where the housing is most fragile. When a diver descends, the seals on the housing are improved with added pressure. In rinse tubs, the camera is not under pressure, and a latch may be opened more easily, resulting in a flood.

# Interacting with Aquatic Life

Learning about how to approach a variety of marine life enhances the enjoyment of underwater photography. Open circuit divers already know that their bubbles tend to alarm fish and marine mammals. Awkward, fast motions will also startle marine life. If you spend your dive chasing things around a reef, you will likely end up with a collection of shots of fish butts. However, if you patiently stake out one location, the marine life may get used to your presence and allow you to get a magical shot. Macro photographers with patience will find that tiny animals like Christmas Tree Worms will come back out of their calcareous home, if they wait patiently for a few minutes without creating any unusual motions. Some animals react with great curiosity to visual stimuli, while others will retreat from unusual water movement, smell or sound.

There are many unique subjects available to shoot at night. Nocturnal animals may not even be visible until well after dark. One of the challenges of night photography is to select the right kind of light for diving. Large primary lights may attract small worms and fish that cloud the ability to get a good shot. Bright lights may also startle nocturnal creatures. Placing a deep red gel over a large light allows the photographer to get close to dark-loving animals while still offering enough illumination for navigation around the reef.

## What to Shoot

The underwater world offers an abundance of subject matter. If you enjoy learning about the small occupants of the reef, then macro photography may be very appealing. If you glory at the wonder of a sheer coral wall, then wide angle photography may fit your interest. Wrecks and caves offer a never ending maze of attractions, but remember the benefits of using a model. Models give a large area, (like a wreck or cave) a sense of scale. Models also allow the viewer to see themselves in the environment. They deliver a sense of wonder and connection with human accomplishment.

## Conservation

The creed among conscientious divers is to take only pictures and leave only bubbles, thus protecting the natural beauty of our underwater world. Photographers should be the very best ambassadors of the environment and should not damage anything for the sake of a photo. This includes physical damage as well as harassment of marine life. One of the greatest objectives of underwater photography is to share a magical world with those that have not had an opportunity to see these rare environments for themselves. As such, it is incumbent on the photographer to be the very best steward of the environment, and improve their diving skills and abilities to their highest level to best protect and sustain the fragile underwater ecosystem.

### Beyond the Reef

Conservation of the underwater environment includes many facets. Biological life, cultural assets, geology, and historical artifacts all deserve to be left as they were found. This includes some items you may not have considered like:

Shipwrecks: They are not only historic artifacts but also precious habitat. As artificial reefs, they may find their greatest calling.

Caves: Delicate speleothems found in submerged cave systems were originally formed when the caves were dry. If broken, these beautiful formations will be forever lost. But, geological formations like rocks, clay banks and sand dunes should also be preserved. They are a part of a unique environment.

Cultural Artifacts: I have been fortunate enough to discover many items of cultural significance. It is imperative that these items be left completely undisturbed. A silt deposit in the eye socket of a skull could yield important information about how long it was submerged. Layers of leaves and detritus may give crucial evidence to a scientist. Never touch or reposition these items for the sake of a photo or critical data will be lost.

## Snake Bite

Nobody is ever around when a snake bites you. I was hovering in a north Florida cave below a popular spot for tubers and snorkelers. The rain had chased everyone out of the water. But as the sky cleared and sun came out, I waited quietly underwater in the mouth of the spring. It was alive, breathing its sweet water skyward.

I was using my Megalodon rebreather; silent, with no bubbles that could defy my presence. My camera was poised, peering upward, knowing it was only a matter of time before an unknowing diver or snorkeler became my model - a perfect silhouette, framed against the blue sky and bracketed by the opening of the cave. It would be spectacular. I waited for what seemed to be an endless twenty minutes knowing that patience would reward a quiet photographer.

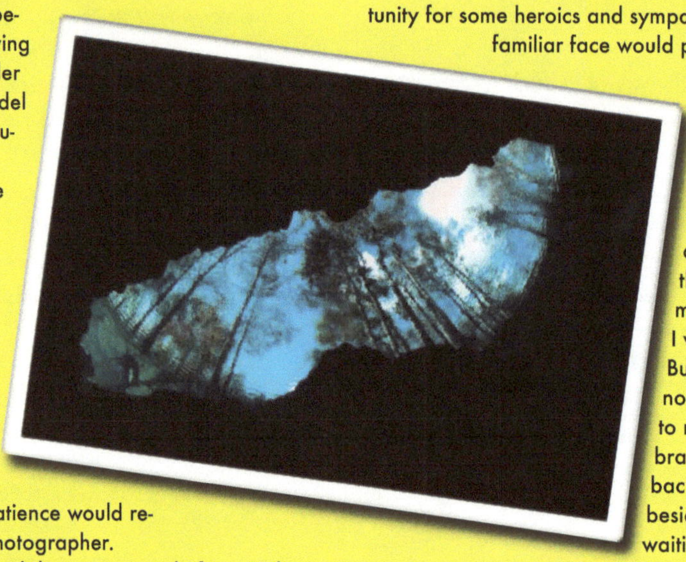

I had experienced these moments before. Hiding in silence for the animals of the woods to reappear. For animals, the passage of time gives them the illusion of safety. Underwater on a soundless rebreather, the surrounding habitat quickly returns to normal. Fish swim around without fear, while you slowly blend, motionless into the environment.

While I awaited my photographic prey, I realized that I was instead the hunted. I felt a needle-like twinge in my middle finger. Instantaneously, I look to my left to see a large brown snake, frightened by my sudden flinch. Was it a Water Moccasin or a harmless Brown Water Snake that had just tasted my juicy finger tip? I squeezed with all my might watching blood stream from the double puncture wound.

I quickly surfaced and climbed out of the water, disappointed that I did not recognize any faces in the parking lot. This wasn't the sort of injury that one wants to experience without the opportunity for some heroics and sympathy. Perhaps a familiar face would pass by before the bleeding stopped.

"Yeah, I got bit by a potentially lethal snake. No big deal. Stuff like this happens to me all the time," I would say.

But there was nobody to listen to my tale of bravery. I paced back and forth beside my van waiting for something monumental to happen. No tingling. No black line extending up my arm. No rotting flesh or swollen appendages. As the bleeding ebbed and the puncture was barely visible, there was nothing left to do but chuckle to myself and head home. I was sitting ready to take a photograph with my finger on the shutter, with the correct exposure set and I didn't even take the shot!.. some professional. Snake bit!

Complementary colors give a vivid boost to any photograph. Use the color wheel on page 57 to see which colors oppose each other on the color wheel. Contrasting these hues adds vibrance to a shot.

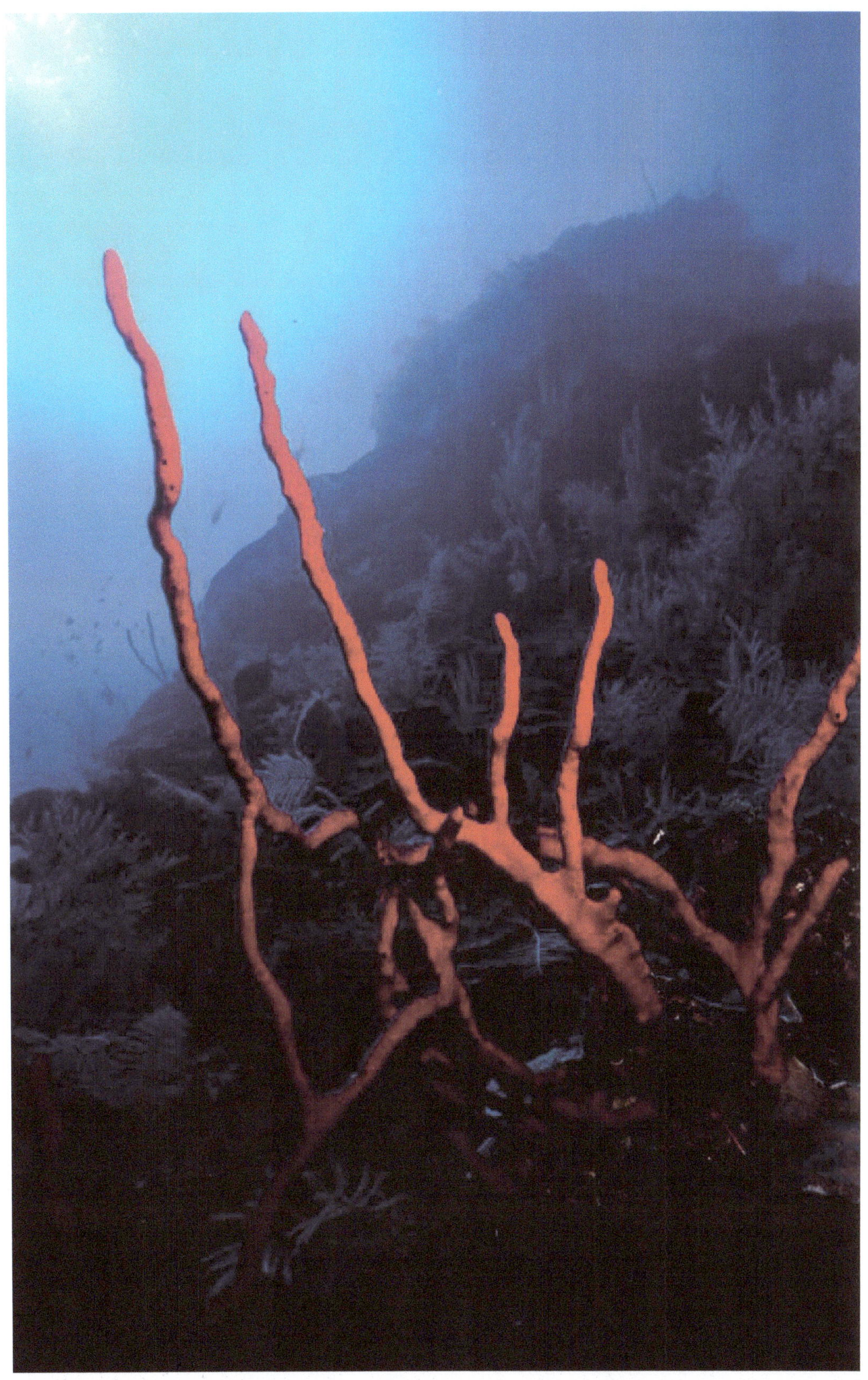

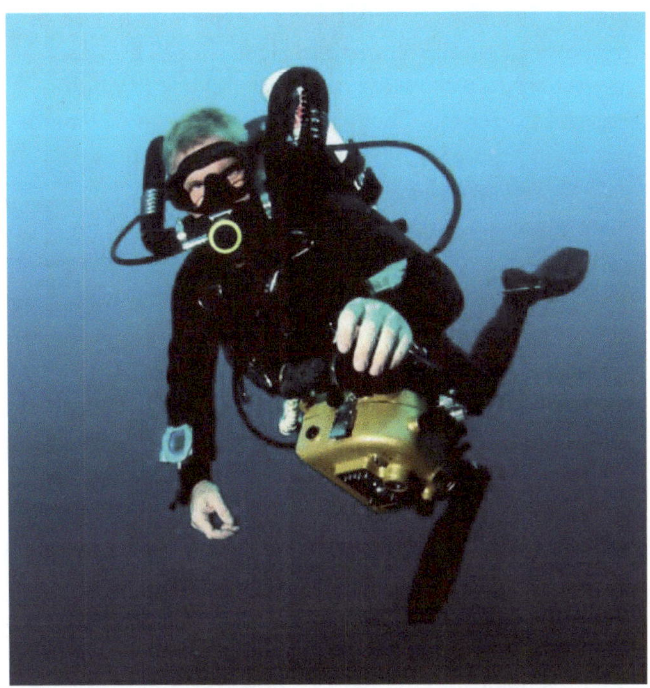

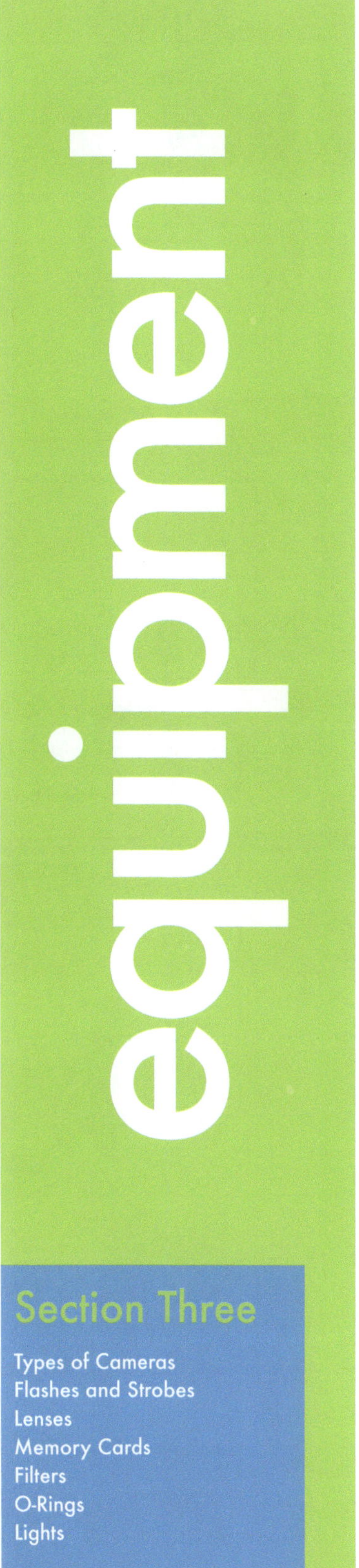


Section Three



## Types of Underwater Cameras

There are currently three common types of digital cameras available for underwater shooting. These are: Compact, Full-Featured Systems and Digital SLR (Single Lens Reflex).

### Compact Cameras

Compact cameras are also often referred to as "point-and-shoot" cameras. These small all-in-one units are designed for easy operation with automatic exposure systems, auto-focussing options and built-in flash units. Compact cameras range from very affordable, disposable versions to more advanced varieties that allow the user some exposure control, zoom, and focus. Many compact cameras offer a wide selection of features, and as the technology improves and costs are reduced, the capabilities of these little cameras continually improve.

The advantage of using a compact camera is that it can be easily stowed in the pocket of a BCD, allowing the diver to carry it along on every dive. The disadvantage of small compact cameras is that they may limit the diver from a full range of shooting opportunities. Compact cameras generally shoot at a lower resolution than more expensive models. They require more light for an exposure and may have a limited frame of ref-

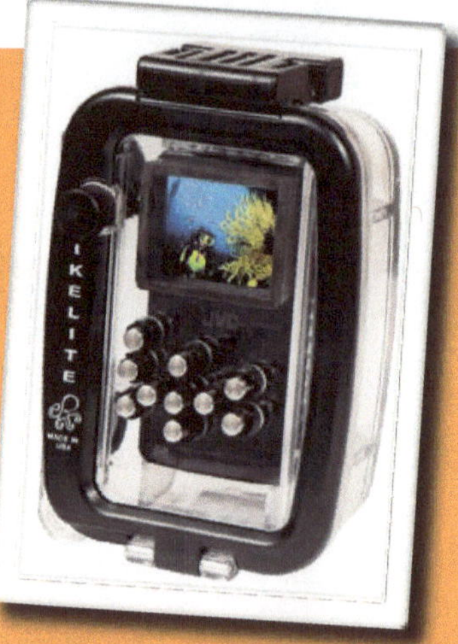


JVC Picsio GC-FM1 combines video and stills in a compact housing.

A compact camera.

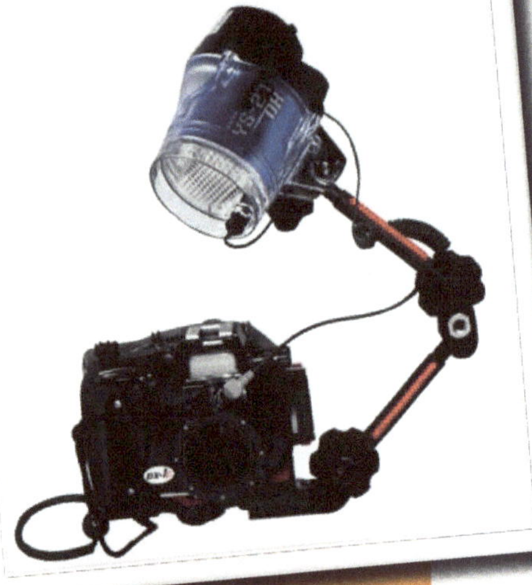

A small Sea and Sea full featured sport package.

erence. The viewfinder for composition may not be as accurate as an SLR camera at close range, but the newest models allow for accurate preview through a digital LCD screen. Shutter-lag on inexpensive cameras may also mean the difference between capturing unique animal behavior and missing the shot completely. Once you understand the limitations of any camera system, you can shoot to optimize its capabilities. The imagination and creative eye of the photographer remains the most valuable feature of any camera system.

Some compact cameras are capable of immersion in shallow diving environments, but to protect the electronics from flooding, most require a pressure vessel, commonly known as a camera housing. These days, almost any digital camera can be housed in a simple plexiglass or Lexan housing. Companies like Ikelite carry a large selection of housings for many popular brands. Ikelite will build a custom housing for almost any camera on the market, however, buying a ready-made housing offers a significant savings. Camera housings are ordinarily priced based on depth rating and the number of features that can be accessed by the photographer underwater. When a depth rating is exceeded, housings either leak, implode or the buttons fail to work properly, generally sticking down in the activated position. In any case, exceeding depth limits of a camera housing will often result in loss of the housing as well as destruction of the camera inside. Electronic cameras are rarely salvageable after a flood, especially in saltwater environments. Familiarize yourself with the housing's capabilities and reduce the chance of a catastrophic failure!

### Full-Featured Camera Systems

Full-featured camera systems fill the niche between compact and SLR cameras. These underwater kits are typically offered with a single, permanently attached lens. The lens may have a range of zoom capability. These systems are often sold with an additional off-camera strobe, increasing the diver's ability to photograph fast-moving fish, and expanding the shooter's creative choices. With a powerful strobe providing artificial light, deeper and darker diving becomes an option.

## Digital SLR Cameras

A single-lens reflex camera features a mirror and prism system that is designed to enable the photographer to look through the attached lens to see precisely what they are shooting. Where a compact camera requires the user to compose using a rangefinder or small LCD screen, the SLR photographer composes the shot by looking directly through the camera lens. This provides the most accurate framing of a shot. Many people are familiar with the 35 mm film version of these cameras, although they are becoming less common.

A Nikon DSLR camera.

Most SLR cameras allow the shooter to select from a variety of detachable lenses. These systems are generally the most expensive, with the price of the SLR system based on lens resolution, shooting features and durability. The most expensive models are equipped with mechanics intended for photographers who will take hundreds of thousands of shots. Most professional photographers prefer the SLR camera systems for reliability, durability, and flexibility. With a pro SLR body, a variety of interchangeable lenses, and a few accessories, almost any underwater photography challenge can be mastered.

The Nikon D300 in a Sea and Sea system housing package.

## Hybrid Cameras

There has recently been an emergence of a new type of camera in the marketplace that will shoot both still and video images. These hybrid cameras are available in most formats, from compact through SLR. Depending on the price, resolution quality, and features, these systems may be capable of doing a good job at both stills and video - or doing neither very well. An understanding of resolution and formats will help a shopper discern the difference.

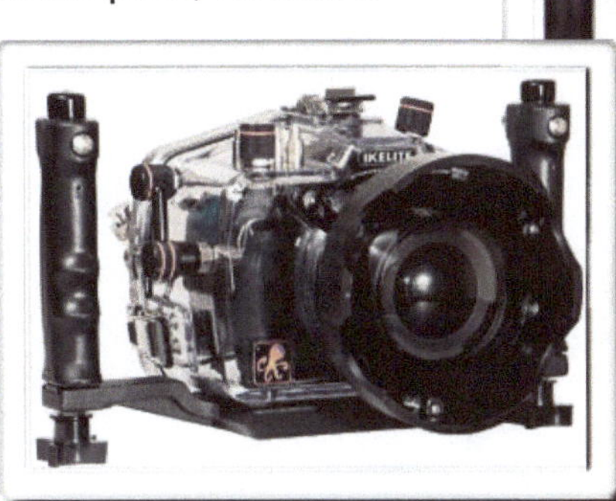

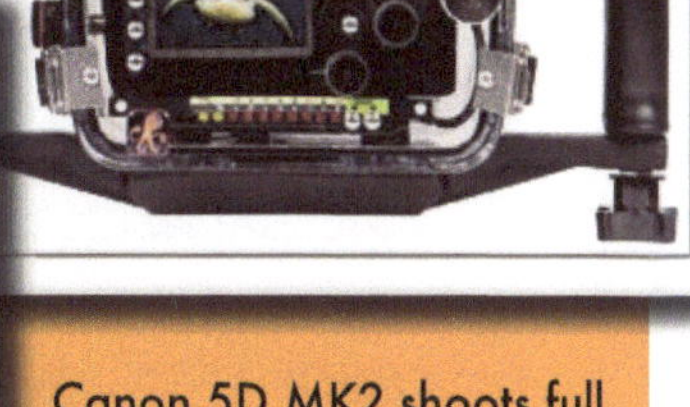

Canon 5D MK2 shoots full HD video and high resolution stills.

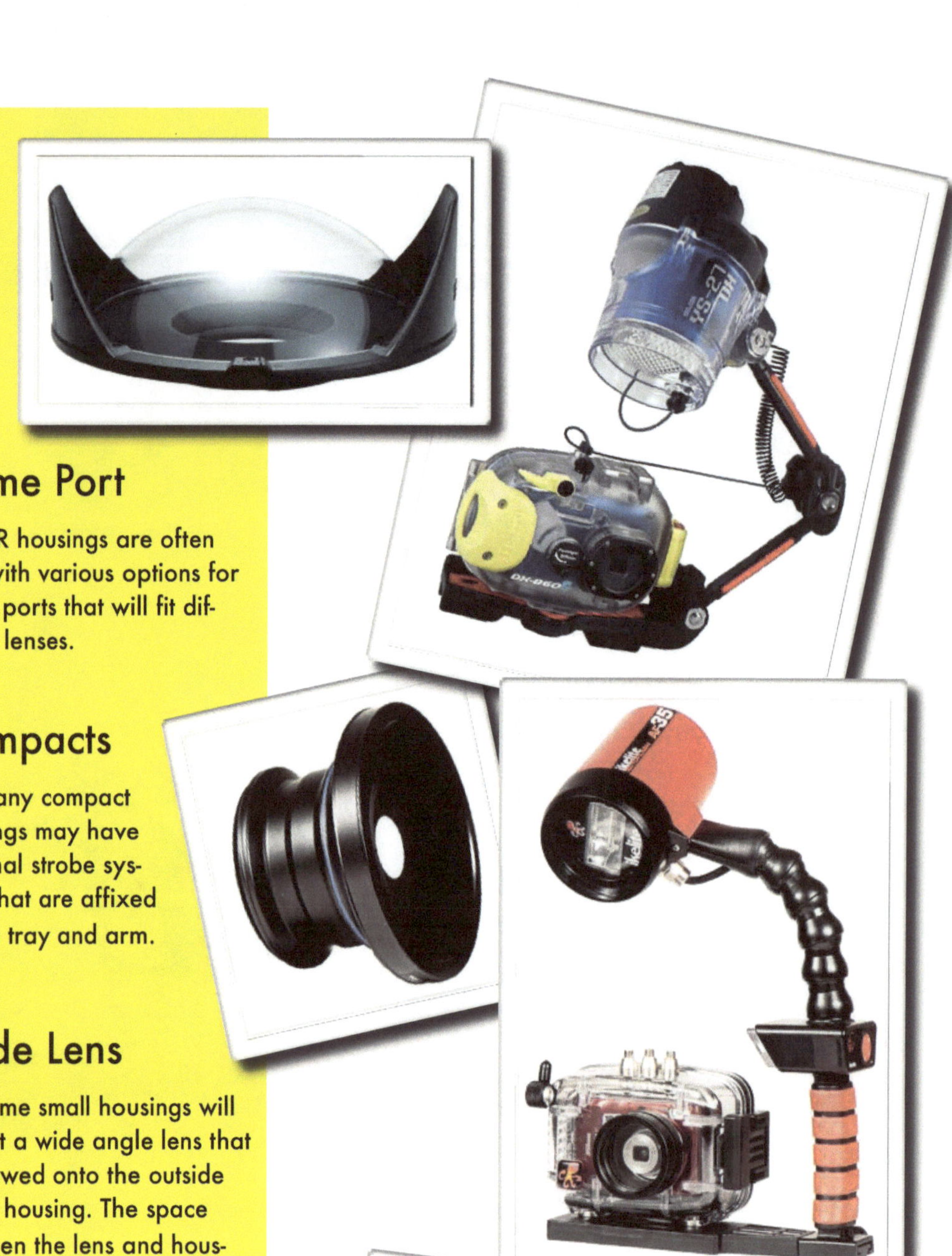

## Dome Port

SLR housings are often sold with various options for dome ports that will fit different lenses.

## Compacts

Many compact housings may have optional strobe systems that are affixed with a tray and arm.

## Wide Lens

Some small housings will accept a wide angle lens that is screwed onto the outside of the housing. The space between the lens and housing is flooded.

## SLR Housing

SLR housings may be manufactured out of clear materials or all-metal bodies. This housing is shown with a tray and handles that accept quick-release strobe arms.

# Flashes and Strobes

Strobes and flash units are used to restore the natural light lost at depth, and enhance the colors that are altered from filtration and absorption. Without strobes, the underwater environment would be a muddy shade of blue.

### Using a Built in Flash

Many compact digital cameras contain a built in flash unit in the body of the camera. Although these are useful for topside flash photography, they can be problematic underwater, causing backscatter. This flash can be masked and used to trigger a second strobe. The flash of light transmits through a fibre optic cable to a remote strobe. This greatly increases capabilities of an otherwise simple camera system.

### Understanding the Capabilities of Your Strobe or Flash Unit

Strobes are specified by a universal power rating called a Guide Number. The guide number describes the output power of the flash unit. A higher guide number, indicates a more powerful strobe.

Your strobe may cost more than your underwater camera and housing. A strobe package will include a strobe head, arms, tray and sync cord or a manual controller and slave sensor. Some strobes operate through fiber-optic cables instead of manual controllers or sync cords.

**Guide Numbers:**
Guide Numbers describe the relative power output of a strobe. They may refer to topside or underwater use and are keyed to film speed. As a result, it is important to convert Guide Numbers to equal parameters before using them for comparison.

## Still Video

In the late 1980s and early 1990s, one of my Toronto advertising clients was the Canon Still Video Division. Still Video was a predecessor to what we know as digital photography today. With this technology, an electronic camera records still images and captures them as single frames of video.

The Xapshot camera had an image sensor that was very similar to camcorders of the time. But, instead of using tape to form a moving image, the data was stored on a disc. In playback mode, the disc could be spun at a fast enough rate to produce a conventional video signal. Additionally, single frames could be extracted by computers that were equipped with a video capture card.

At the time, Canon and Sony thought they had a technology that would change the marketplace. However, news photographers were taking the digital imagery one step further by editing beyond the truth. At the time, there was great controversy over baseballs that were moved into catcher's mitts or flab rolls that were nipped from the hips of runway models. It was unclear whether digital photography would ever be accepted by the public, let alone by law enforcement or other institutional applications.

These days, film cameras are considered vintage and film is difficult, if not impossible to find. Kodak has ceased production of most of its film products. Still Video was way ahead of its time, paving the way for the newest wave of emerging technology, which provides the photographer with the ability to make very high resolution stills and, incredibly, full HD video at the same time.

Entry-level strobes are usually powered with Alkaline batteries while more capable units are powered with rechargeable NiMh or Lithium Ion packs. The specifications for your strobe will describe how many flashes you will get with a given power supply and how quickly the unit will recycle and fire again.

If you plan to photograph low light scenarios like caves, wrecks or night dives, it takes a serious investment in strobe power to shoot anything more than the most simple snapshots. Without sufficient artificial light in these challenging, dark environments, low power flash cameras can do little more than produce a headshot on a dark background.

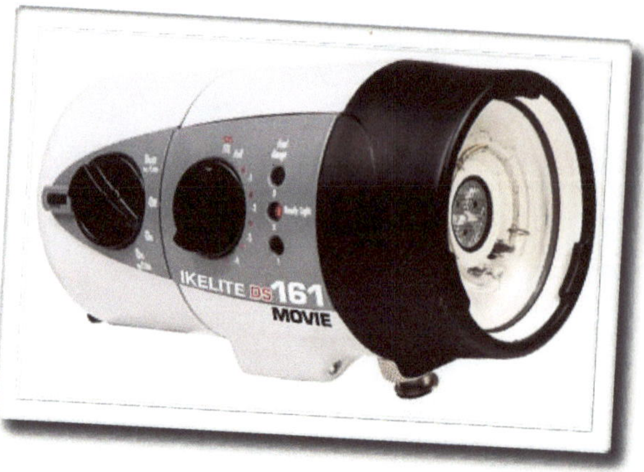


The term strobe refers to a lighting unit that is independent from the camera (seen above). The term flash refers to a lighting unit that is built in to the camera, inside the housing.

## Lenses

Many digital cameras give the user the ability to zoom in closer to a subject. There are two types of zoom capabilities offered in integrated lenses – digital zoom and optical zoom.

Digital zoom is really a misnomer and not a true zoom at all. Digital zoom simply magnifies an image on your screen and enlarges the pixels. As you zoom in digitally, you lose resolution and sharpness and the picture looks fuzzy.

True optical zoom means that the camera is capable of changing the focal length of the lens by shifting the distance between several pieces of optical glass inside the lens. As these lens elements shift, the apparent field of view of the image changes. With adjustable focal length, or "zoom" lenses, the photographer can either take a wide-angle shot of a coral reef or zoom in close for a picture of a starfish.

By carefully examining a specification sheet, you can review the degree of optical and digital zoom offered with a particular model.

Long-range zoom features do not have much practicality underwater, since they prevent the diver from getting close to the subject. If you are able to safely approach a subject and shoot at close range, you will minimize the column of light- and color-filtering water between the camera and subject. If you shoot further away and zoom in, you may be able to get good animal behavior, but the shot quality is degraded by the water filtering effects.

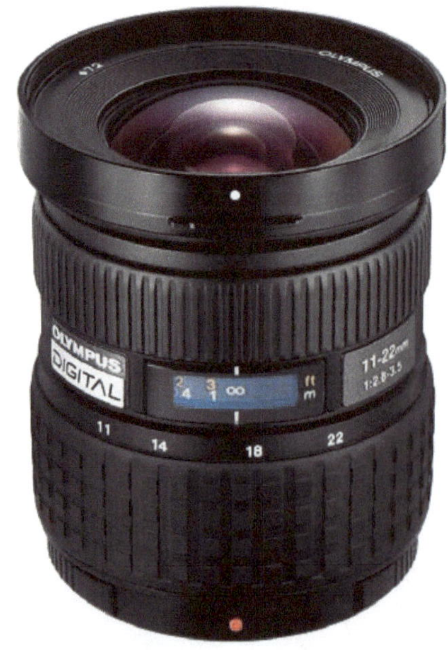

## Lenses for Digital SLR Cameras

Lenses are described by their focal length - fisheye, wide angle, normal, and telephoto. Most underwater photographers seek out wide-angle lenses to couple with their digital SLR (DSLR) camera. Wide-angle lenses help the photographer to get close to the subject and minimize the amount of light- and color-filtering water between the camera and the subject. Telephoto lenses are not useful in the underwater environment because of reasons described above. It is not practical to take a long distance photo through light-filtering water that is often filled with particulate.

Fixed focal length lenses are known as prime lenses. Variable focal length lenses are referred to as zoom lenses. Lenses are also rated for speed, which is a numerical value based on the largest possible aperture, or iris opening. A "fast" lens is one that allows the photographer to select a smaller f-stop number like f/1.4. The lower the f-stop number, the larger the aperture opening. This can be confusing, but just remember that a small number represents a bigger opening, and a big number represents a smaller opening. An f-stop of f/1.4 allows more light to strike the image area than an f-stop of f/2.8. A slow lens will be rated with a higher f-stop number like f/4. The faster a lens is rated, the more functional it will be in lower light conditions. Divers should try to get as fast a lens as they can afford, since most underwater scenarios are light-deprived. Another variable in selecting a lens is whether it can be automatically focused, or whether it only allows for manual focus operation. Finally, lenses are rated as professional when they are durably built, to meet the demands of changing environments, and with extremely high quality, polished glass elements.

### Aperture

The aperture, or iris, in a lens is much like the human eye. The larger the opening, the more light reaches the camera sensor.

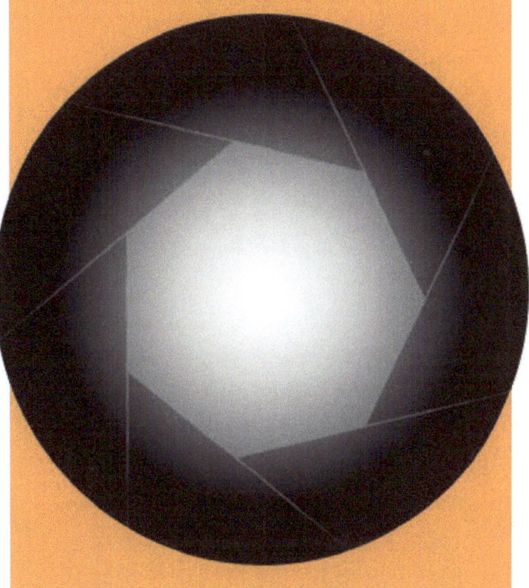

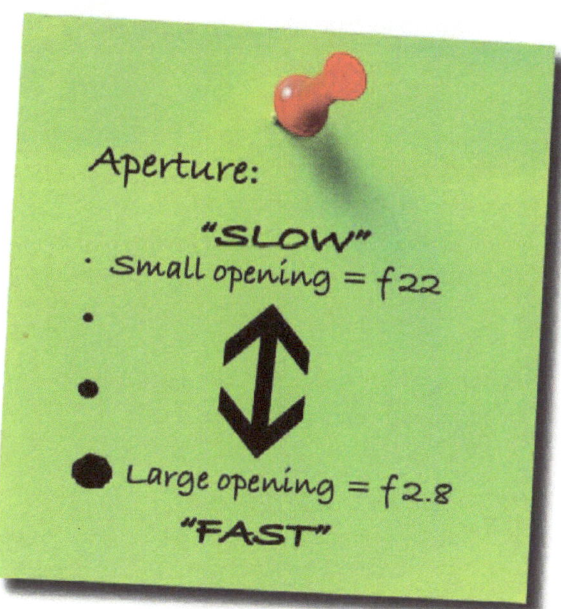


Some DSLR cameras, such as some models of Nikon, use a digital sensor area that is smaller than the equivalent image area of 35 mm film. There are advantages and disadvantages to this feature, depending on what type of shooting you like to do. Older and standard Nikon lenses behave differently on film cameras than their digital counterparts. The sensor image area in some Nikon DSLR cameras is cropped by a factor of about 1.5 times. That means that a wildlife photographer who owns a standard 200 mm telephoto lens will find that it has the equivalent focal length of a 300 mm lens, when used with a DSLR camera body. Standard SLR lens distances are significantly enhanced when coupled to a DSLR with a cropped sensor. On the other hand, people who love shooting wide-angle shots discover a narrower field of view when they put their old 17-35 mm on their new digital camera. This lens has the equivalent field of view of a 26-52 mm lens on a cropped sensor. Newer Nikon lenses labeled "DX" give true focal lengths (similar to those of a 35 mm SLR) based on the cropped sensor.

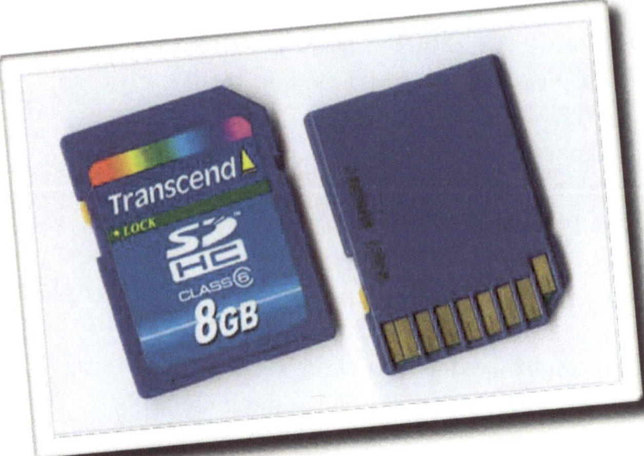


More recently, Nikon, Canon and other camera companies have begun to feature full-frame sensors. These cameras offer a sensor image area that is equivalent in size to a 35 mm film stock. If you own DX or other cropped-sensor lenses, the image becomes cropped, but standard lenses operate to their full and best capacity.

Finally, an even more advanced type of lens is entering the arena. Manufacturers are now developing speciality lenses with enhanced optics, that are designed for the unique needs of the digital realm.

## Memory Cards

Memory cards come in various formats like Compact Flash (CF), Microdrive (MD), Smart Media, Secure Disk (SD), Memory Stick, floppy disk, and CD. Each camera model has a specific type of memory card that will fit in its memory slot. Considering the needs of the photo shoot, underwater photographers can choose the storage capacity of the camera's memory card. Of course, larger capacity cards are best for effective shooting and image file management.

Microdrives are very small hard drives packaged inside the body of a Compact Flash memory card. Since Microdrives have moving mechanical parts, they can be fragile. They use air to float the heads of the drive and therefore cannot be used at altitudes above 10,000 feet. The recording head can be damaged and data may be permanently lost.

Cameras are often packaged with very small memory cards, which are only large enough to take a few pictures for demonstration and setup of the camera. It is a good idea to purchase at least two additional cards so that one can be swapped out when downloading is not convenient.

Memory cards come in capacity ranges from 512 kilobytes to 12 gigabytes and they are getting larger all the time. Cards that are 2 gigabytes or larger use a special image filing system that is specific to higher-end cameras. Check your camera's specifications to find out whether it can read and write to a large card.

Some manufacturers rate their cards by speed. This rating specifies how quickly data can be written to a card and how quickly it can be retrieved. Sports photographers prefer very fast cards and cameras with large buffers to catch peak action and special moments like a touchdown pass. Some underwater photographers find fast cards useful for capturing the unique moments of animal behaviors that happen only once in a lifetime.

The number of images that may be stored on a card is a direct relationship to the file size of the photos that are shot. Most cameras will allow the photographer to select the image quality and resulting file size. In almost all cases, underwater photographers will use the finest/highest image quality setting available on their camera.

**Buffer:**
In order to reduce the delay between shots, the memory buffer temporarily holds the data until the image is processed and written to the memory card for storage.

## Filters

Red filters are used by some divers in open water scenarios that are too vast to light with strobes. When enough ambient light is available, a red filter can restore natural color to scenes that are too large to fill with a flash. Large wrecks and caverns are good subjects in which to apply this technique. The filter blocks the blue and green tints and enhances the reds, oranges and yellows. They can only be used without a flash, since adding a flash would defeat the filter and cause the photo to appear too red.

### The Pencil Holder

When you pursue the art of underwater photography, you will eventually experience a loss from flooding. In the early years, I used to carefully bathe the afflicted gear in alcohol and send it off to a repair facility with the naive hope that something could be salvaged. There was an expert repair tech in Texas who often covered my service needs. He was very good, but his repairs were usually accompanied by nasty notes. To him, these masterpieces of technology deserved the care and protection afforded a sentient being. Accusations of "how could you?" admonished owners for abuse of their Nikonos cameras. But, if anyone could save a flood, he could.

I packaged up a flooded camera in an alcohol bath, attempting to prevent the crystallization of salt through the unit. I shipped the sealed cooler to Texas, hoping the package would not leak along the way. Days later I received a terse letter with a checklist of options for repair. The cheeky tech charged me almost a hundred dollars to make nothing more sophisticated than a desk-worthy pencil holder out of my Nikonos V camera. I loved it.

## O-rings

O-rings create the barrier between your precious camera and the treacherous underwater world. Proper care of O-rings is essential to protect your investment. They should be carefully removed from the housing with a blunt object like a credit card or pinched, stretched and popped from their groove. They should be carefully cleaned and lightly lubricated with silicone grease. The main door and port O-rings should be removed from the housing for long term storage so they do not "take a set" or conform to a shape, referred to as "memory." When traveling, it is imperative they are either out of the housing or the housing is blocked open. Housings are designed to withstand positive pressure from submersion, but are not designed to survive pressure reductions caused when flying in airplanes. Buttons may become damaged and in extreme cases, housing controls will explode outwards in airline baggage. O-rings should be immediately replaced if they are damaged and should be swapped out annually for preventive maintenance.

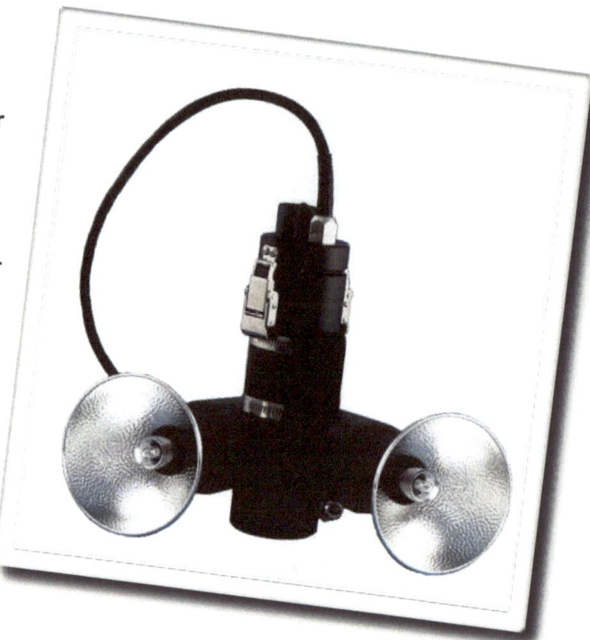

Large video reflectors will soften and diffuse the light so that it does not appear as a hot spot in your shot. Other purpose-built focus lights will dim when your strobe fires.

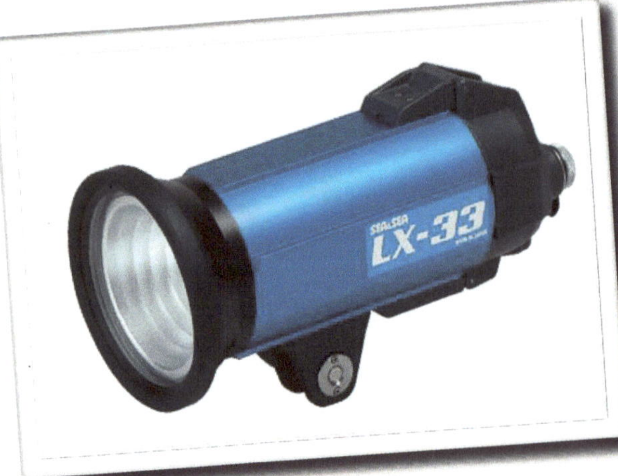


Video lights, such as this Sea and Sea model, are good diffused lighting for fill or key lighting.

## Focus Lights

Focus lights are used to help the photographer manually focus or offer enough light for the auto-focus function to operate. Some strobes have built-in focus lights that emit a soft, diffused light. These focus lights actually dim when the strobe fires so that they do not show up in the photograph. Specialty retailers also offer independent focus lights with a very diffuse coverage of light. Standard dive lights are not appropriate, since they often leave a glaring hot spot or an unattractive beam in the shot.

Video lights may be used as focus lights as long at the video light has a soft diffuser that covers the full area of the particular lens you are using.

Focus lights may be mounted on the camera housing with a ball joint and saddle or they may be strapped to the side of a strobe if not built in.

## Other Lights

Cave and wreck diving primary lights such as HID's, offer a tremendous amount of brightness, but are not ordinarily diffused enough to assist in photography. They mimic the color temperature of sunlight. If you add a video reflector or white diffuser, these lights can be converted to helpful key lights that may be used by the photographer as a focus light or to add a little brightness to the foreground or to a diver's mask. They are very complimentary to a standard color balance, since their output is very close to daylight at around 5500° K. Lights are rated in degrees Kelvin (K) to help compare their relative color. This is the same scale that denotes white balance, which is described in detail later in the text.

## Equipment for Models

Whether you are the photographer or the model, your personal dive gear should be trimmed carefully to avoid entanglements or damaging the environment. Models, in particular, should be depicted with the appropriate safe configuration for the type of diving they are undertaking. As a photographer whose images may be published, you have a responsibility to show divers engaging in safe practices with the correct equipment. Publishing a shot of a diver kneeling on a reef will set back years of good work of conservation organizations. Depicting an open water diver in a cave without proper equipment or technique, may encourage unsafe practices. It is your job as the photographer to make sure your subjects are "squared away."

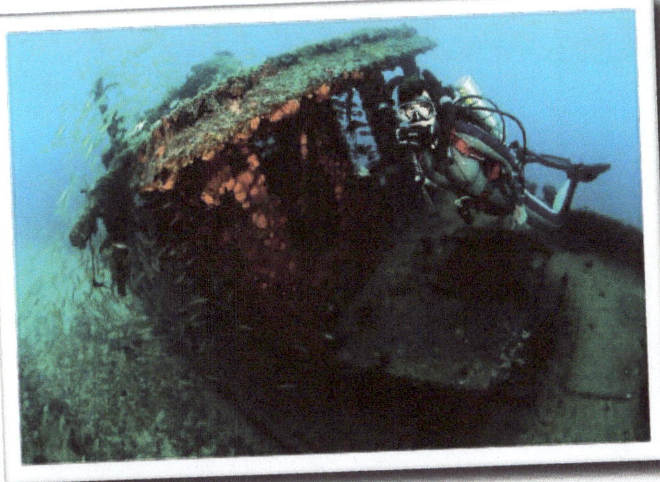

### Color Temperature

Color temperature refers to the degree of whiteness in light and is measured in degrees Kelvin.

| | |
|---|---|
| **6800** | **COOL LIGHT** |
| **6600** | **Electronic Flash** |
| **6400** | |
| **6200** | |
| **6000** | **Cloudy Haze** |
| **5800** | |
| **5600** | **HID** |
| **5400** | **Daylight** |
| **5200** | |
| **5000** | **Noon Sun** |
| **4800** | |
| **4600** | |
| **4400** | |
| **4200** | **Fluorescent** |
| **4000** | |
| **3800** | |
| **3600** | |
| **3400** | |
| **3200** | |
| **3000** | **Halogen** |
| **2800** | **Incandescent** |
| **2600** | **Early Sun** |
| **2400** | **WARM LIGHT** |

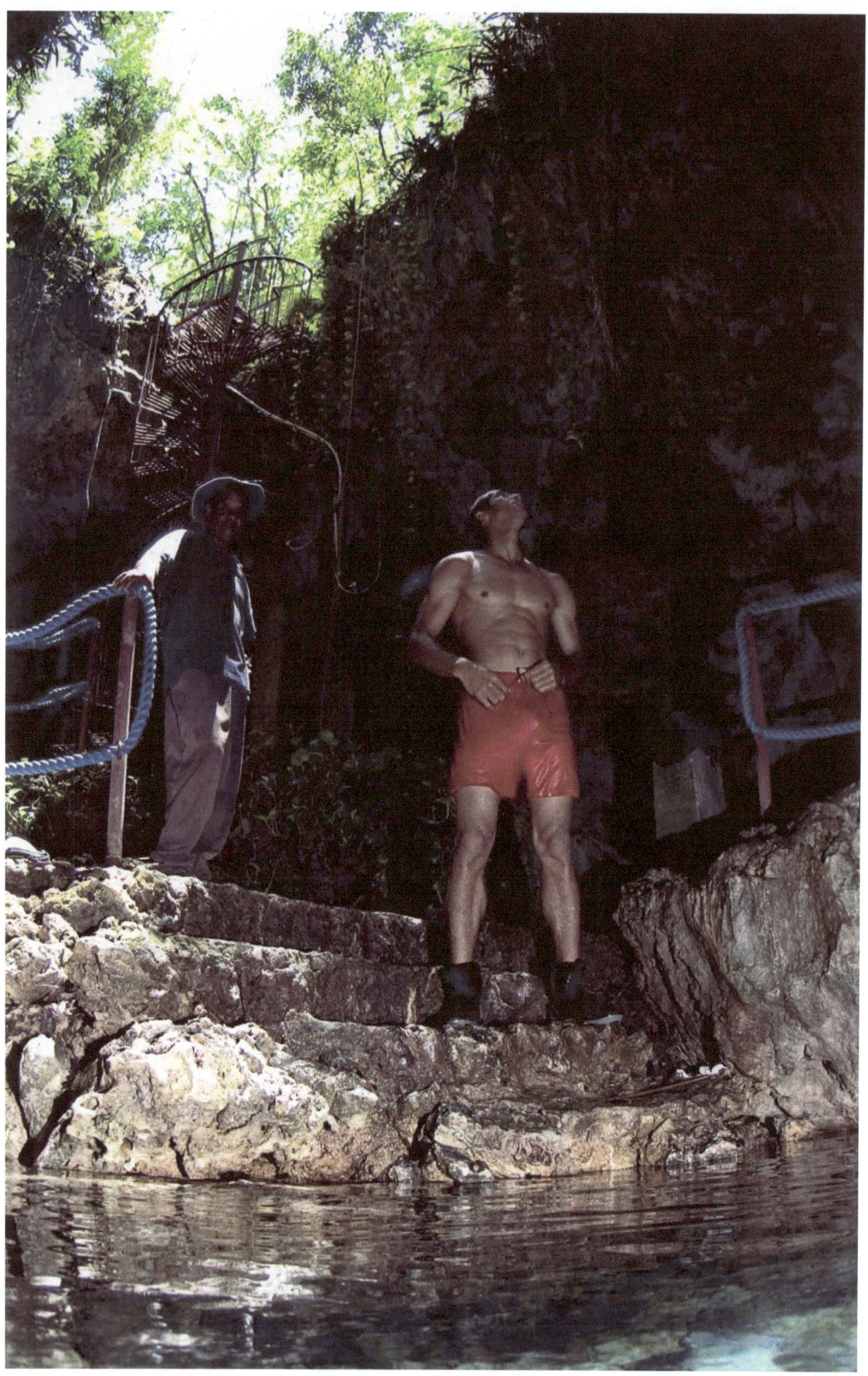

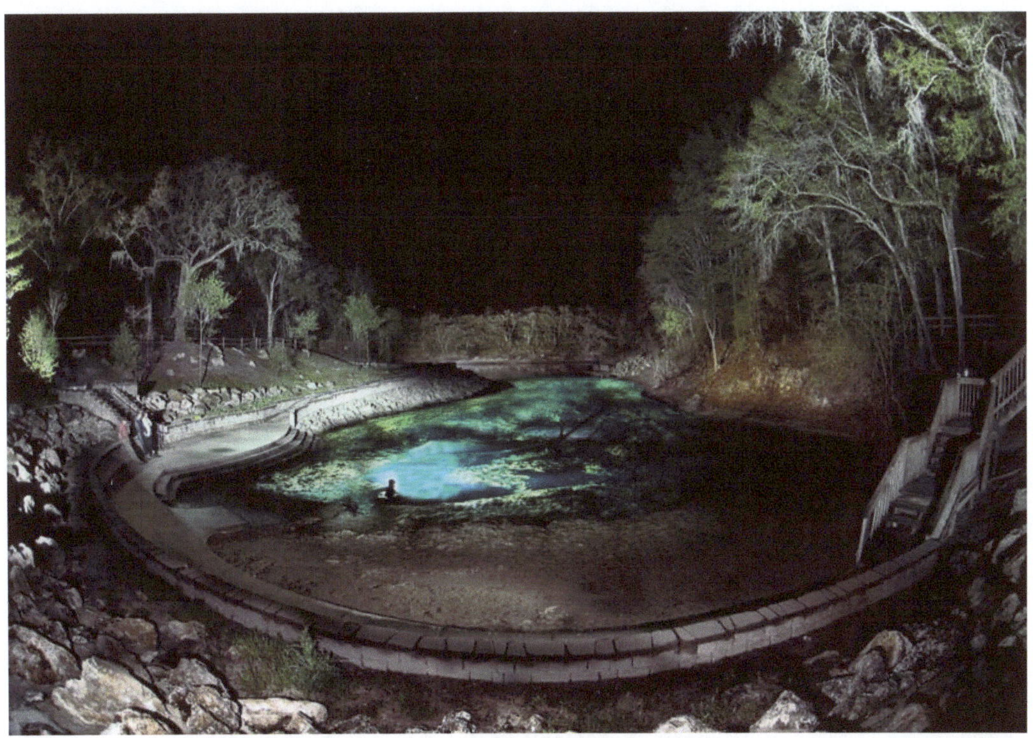

The photo on the facing page was taken in the water, right at water level. The water actually laps up on the edge of the dome port.

The photo of a Florida spring above was taken with a technique I call "painting." In this shot, I use several manually operated underwater strobes, an HID light and a very long exposure. If you notice the diver in the water, he is also leaning against the wall. The same assistant is in the shot twice through overlapping, multiple exposures. This landscape took several hours to illuminate.

the dive

## Section Four

Camera Prep
Buddy Planning
Entries and Exits
Changeovers
Post Dive Care
Sensor Cleaning

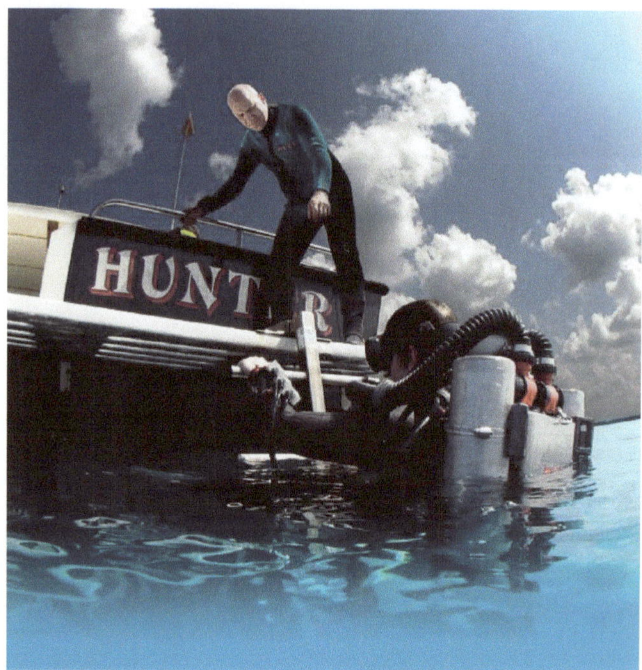


## Camera Prep and Testing

Before you do anything else, check to ensure that you have a freshly formatted, empty memory card in your camera. Check that your battery life is adequate to get through your dive day and recharge if necessary. Carefully clean the camera lens using lens tissue or a specialized lens cloth. Never use towels or clothing to clean a camera lens as it may become irreparably scratched. If there is a stubborn stain or grease on the lens, place a couple of drops of lens cleaner on a lens tissue and then rub the lens. Do not drop cleaning fluid directly on the camera lens.

Carefully inspect the camera housing and dome port for damage and dirt. The interior of the housing must be free of dirt, hair and grease that can end up in front of the lens. Canned air or even a scuba tank with a low pressure nozzle may be used to carefully remove dirt from the interior of a housing.

Thoroughly inspect and clean all O-rings according to the manufacturer's instructions. They should never be removed with anything sharp, since they can be easily damaged.

Use a small amount of silicone lubricant to put a slight sheen on O-rings. Never use excessive amounts since it may cause leakage.

Place the camera in the housing according to the manufacturer's directions. Follow instructions carefully. The camera should not be difficult to install in the housing if all the buttons are in the correct position. Incorrect assembly can result in damaged buttons and levers or eventual leakage.

Assemble the strobe units and arms according to the manufacturer's instructions and angle the strobes toward the subject.

Turn on the camera and strobes. Test the focus and other buttons for proper function. Fire a test shot to ensure functionality of the strobe units or slaves.

Place the camera in a rinse tank to test for leaks before diving, or carefully place the camera in the water if entering from shore. If the housing has a leak detector, ensure the camera is powered on and listen for the beep or look for the leak detector light to ensure everything is fine. Bubbles escaping from any part of the system, means that water is getting in to your housing or strobe. If so, remove immediately and hold the housing in a way that lessens the likelihood of water touching the camera itself.

If you are entering the water by giant stride or back roll, have someone pass the camera down to you in the water. Jumping or rolling into the water with a camera may result in immediate, catastrophic flooding.

## Buddy Planning

Prior to the dive, ensure that your buddy is completely aware of their role as model or safety officer. If you make the dive buddy an active part of the shoot, they will stay engaged in the process and contribute to a safer environment. Review signals and refresh your buddy about any shots you would like to set up. Coach them on body position and trim. Remind them to be vigilant in helping you keep track of gas supplies and dive plans. Advise them to notify you if your position might cause damage to the environment.

### The 80 lb. Parka

Airline baggage limitations are getting more stringent every day. There was a time when I could fly on a media pass and take unlimited extras for $25 a piece, up to 100 pounds. I recall one instance where I flew from LA to Washington, London and Bucharest with 28 pieces and a $3500 bill for extra baggage. Now, extra baggage is nearly impossible.

A few years back, I flew to Ekaterinberg, Russia, at a time when baggage embargoes were strict. I needed to travel to the edge of Siberia with a video package, photo gear, cave diving equipment and something to keep me warm for a couple of weeks. The biggest challenge was the weight limitation. I was allowed two, fifty pound bags and a single carry on. This was clearly going to be impossible, so I took the heaviest batteries and regulators and lenses and loaded them in my wheeled carry-on case. I could hardly lift it onto the inspection conveyor. But, as the airlines had no "wear-it-on" limitations, I decided to pack as much dive and camera gear as humanly possible into the pockets, nooks and crannies of my Antarctic parka. I wore several layers of clothing and my heavy winter boots as I embarked on the plane in balmy Florida. Once safely seated, I began to strip down layers and deposited them in a folding shopping bag I had stuffed in a pocket. On arrival in London, I donned the bulky layers again, heaved my heavy parka laden with goodies over my shoulders and shuffled through international security.

As I approached the x-ray, I began removing all the layers and boots and placed them in the plastic bins. Laptop in one. Boots in another. Parka overflowing. Six bins later, I walked through the metal detector and got patted down for looking so heavily stuffed.

Beyond the x-ray I had to empty every pocket of the 80 lb. parka and explain my way through security. Rather than being annoyed, the affable British officers were easily amused by my persistence and strength.

As I struggled down the aisle on my Moscow connection, I was relieved to discover that my carry-on fit in the overhead bin. The 40 kilo limit obviously exceeded by my single bag, I took a risk and heaved the overloaded parka into the tray and settled into my seat for the next leg of travel. It's no wonder flying is so tiring. It's a workout.

## Getting in the Water

After the camera has been passed to you in the water, check all functions and look for bubbles. As you descend, check the dome port for small micro bubbles and gently rub them off to clear the lens. Be careful of rings on your hands that could scratch the dome!

## Exiting the Water

When you are ready to leave your safety stop, check the housing carefully for anything that does not appear to be seated properly like battery doors, lens ports or cable fittings. Anything loose will stay in place at fifteen feet, but as pressure is reduced and surface conditions bounce the diver and housing around, the greatest risk of flooding occurs.

As soon as possible, pass the camera to topside personnel, carefully showing them what part of the housing they may safely grab. Ask them to gently place the camera on deck so that you can put it in the rinse tank yourself and guard against dome port scratches.

## Changeovers

If you need to switch memory cards or batteries before your next dive, care should be taken to dry the camera as much as possible. Ensure your body is dry enough that you do not drip water into an open housing or camera. Pull down your exposure suit to your waist and put a towel on your head to prevent such mishaps.

When opening a housing or strobe on a boat or near water, plan to open the housing in a direction that will protect the interior from dripping water. Allow the water to run down and off of the housing. Use a towel to drape over yourself and the camera so that spray from divers and waves do not get into the system. Ensure the camera is turned off. With dry hands, carefully replace the batteries or card and immediately close the housing, watching carefully for pinched O-rings. Safeguard used cards in a small waterproof case.

Follow the prep and test procedures, described previously, to ensure that all elements of the camera are still properly aligned in the housing.

## Post Dive Care

Immediately after a saltwater dive, you can use a spray bottle of Salt-X to prevent encrustation of minerals on the housing. As soon as possible, soak the camera housing in freshwater and depress all the buttons to guarantee thorough rinsing. Turn the strobe dials on and off to get all the salt out of the controls.

Freshwater dives and pool sessions may also necessitate immediate washing of your camera housing. The dome port of the housing may develop hazing or mineral spots if left unrinsed. These deposits may be impossible to remove if allowed to dry fully.

Mineral deposits are like wet concrete. They are very easy to rinse and remove when wet and almost impossible to wash away after they have set.

### Explosion

Did you know that a camera housing that is closed up tight in airline baggage can explode? It doesn't exactly blow to pieces, but a button or port may fail and breach the waterproof integrity of the unit.

Always travel with a door open or o-rings removed.

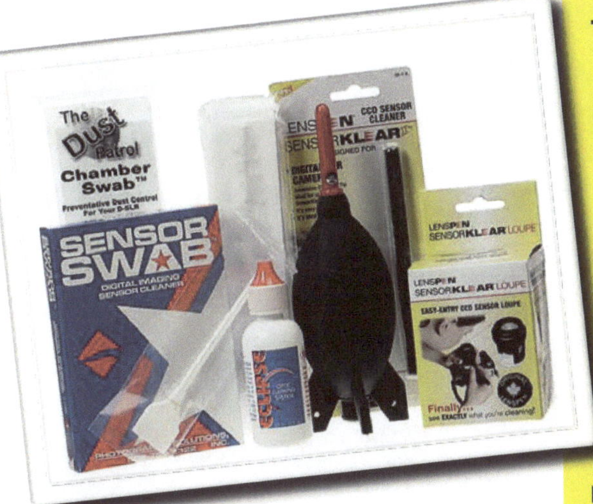


## Sensor Cleaning

Many SLR cameras feature an auto sensor cleaning function that removes dust from the image sensor inside the camera. Sensor dust may be prevented by waiting five-seconds after turning off the camera, before changing lenses. The sensor plate is energized when the camera is on. It holds a charge of static electricity that sucks dust into the camera body when it is on and open. If allowed to rest for several seconds, the static will be discharged before the camera body is breached for lens changes.

In the event that your sensor develops a dirt spot, this can either be removed in careful editing or the sensor may be carefully hand cleaned. Sensor swabbing is a delicate process. It must be done with the correct materials or the camera can be ruined. Many online photography retailers carry sensor swab kits with proper instructions for cleaning. Follow your camera manufacturer's guidelines if you have the need to manually clean the image sensor! Some manufacturers and repair facilities offer annual cleaning and repair services if you feel uncomfortable about doing this yourself. Ensure that you seek out a reputable firm to take on this delicate task.

## The Best Shots I Never Took

On completion of the United States Deep Caving Team's Wakulla Project in 1999, I was asked to send my slides to National Geographic for consideration in upcoming articles. I was excited that they were going to take a look at my work. For this special magazine project, I decided that I would not risk using my local film lab for processing. Instead, I would send my large bag of exposed rolls directly to Kodak. I had done this before with bulk quantities and assumed that they could offer the best service in the industry. I was anxious to see my shots and dupes, but even more anxious to get the originals up to National Geographic. I waited for what seemed to be a long time and called Kodak headquarters in Rochester to inquire about delivery. I was told they were in process. After a couple of weeks, I got worried. My daily inquiries were getting nowhere. I begged for somebody to give me the news and told them about how important these images could be to my career. Finally, after almost three weeks, a large UPS envelope arrived at my house. I quickly ripped open the edge and found 27 letters with coupons attached, each apologizing for the loss of my film. The coupon, good for a replacement roll of film, was somehow supposed to make me feel better. The project had represented three months of my life, unpaid. My home had been burglarized and cleaned out during the expedition, my marriage was suffering and somehow this was supposed to make me feel better. In the end, I had a single roll of film, shot from the 1997 test runs at Wakulla. A single roll yielded a single publishable image for me. Somehow, I'd like to think that those 27 lost rolls represent some of the most interesting and rare shots I have ever taken. Any wonder why I have so lovingly embraced digital underwater photography?

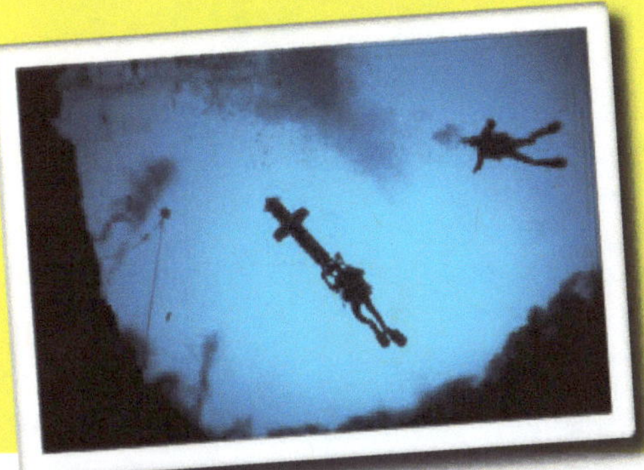

# physics

## Section Five

File Types
Metadata and EXIF
Resolution
Exposure Theory
Film Speed
Depth of Field

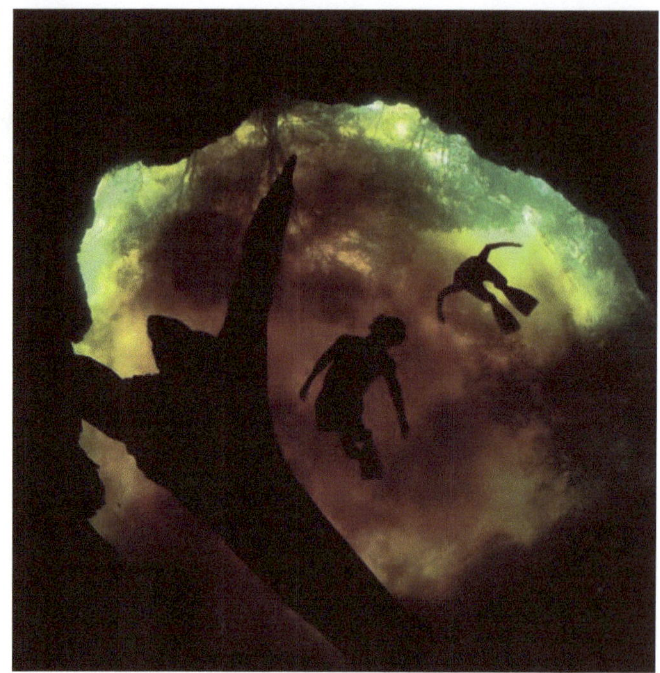

## File Types

Many cameras permit the shooter to select from a variety of file formats for shooting as well as a variety of resolutions. Lower resolution files are easier to email and store and allow the user to pack a lot more onto a memory card. Higher resolution files take up more space, but may be later downsized for use in other applications.

It is important to understand the different types of files since each offers advantages and disadvantages for shooting and storage.

### JPEG Files

JPEG stands for Joint Photographic Experts Group. This is likely the most popular file format for photographers for the following reasons:

Files are very small and highly compressed allowing for the maximum number of images stored on a given card. This in turn saves memory. JPEGs write quickly from the memory buffer to the memory card. JPEG files are ready to view without any processing and also ready to email. Many of these images are optimized by programs in the camera, correcting for exposure errors. JPEGs are universal for file sharing compatibility and they easily transfer through the Internet and email applications.

The disadvantage of using the JPEG file format is that critical data is lost forever when a file is compressed. Each subsequent time a JPEG photo is opened and saved, even more data can be lost. You can usually manipulate a JPEG photo once or twice before it becomes unusable. Lost data often results in something called compression artifacts. These undesirable changes in the photographic file are a result of camera optics and processing. Low resolution JPEGs will also have "jaggies" that look like stair-stepping on obvious diagonal lines. They result from the square layout of the pixels. The more you magnify this image, the more "jaggies" you will see. Finally, JPEGs may look softer overall, less sharp than TIFFs and RAW files.

### TIFF Files

TIFF stands for Tagged Image File Format. This format results in a very high image quality that does not degrade when opened, manipulated and saved. This is called "lossless compression." This file format is fairly universal in the printing industry. These images do not require any specialty software and are therefore immediately usable straight out of the camera.

The disadvantage of TIFF files are that they are very large. They take time to write from the buffer to the card and fill up your memory card quickly, delaying your opportunity to take a follow-up shot. Although they are immediately usable straight out of the camera, they are often too large to email. Although common in the printing industry, other computer users may not have a program capable of viewing TIFF files.

### RAW Files

These files are completely unprocessed and consist of all the data gathered at the image sensor. This is the virtual equivalent to an undeveloped film negative. RAW files offer the best opportunities for image manipulation and the highest quality available from the camera.

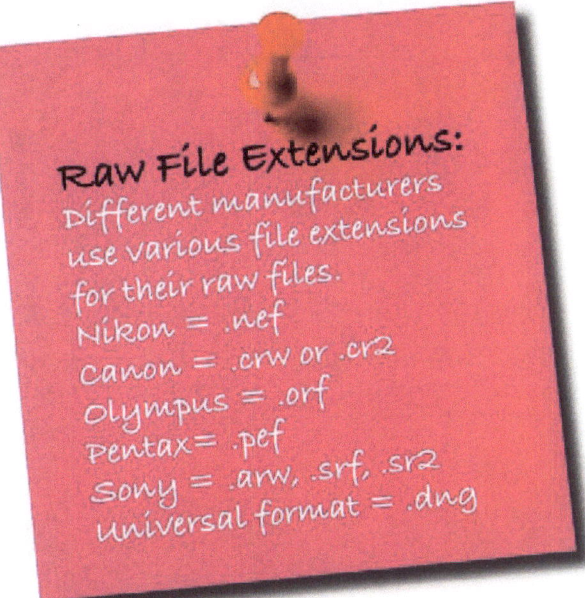


All camera images begin as pure RAW files. JPEGs are simply RAW files that are processed inside the camera for things like white balance, exposure, sharpness, color balance, compression, etc.

The advantage of shooting in RAW is that you have total control over the image after you shoot. RAW files are loaded into your computer where they can be manipulated with much more powerful image processing software programs than are available in your camera. Each pixel in a high-end SLR may have 4000 possible levels of brightness as opposed to a JPEG file where each pixel has been dummied down to one of 256 levels. Although they will look identical on your computer screen (which only displays 256 levels of brightness) the adjustability of a RAW image is far greater in programs such as Aperture, Lightroom or Photoshop.

The drawback is that RAW files are large (though not as large as TIFFs). They increase write time and reduce space on your memory card. RAW file extensions differ from camera to camera and a camera-specific RAW converter is needed to open the files. This means that a RAW

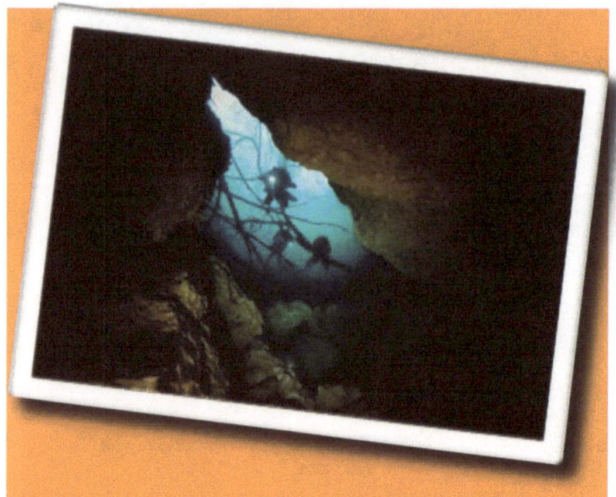

**SAMPLE EXIF DATA**

F/2.8
1/60
ISO 200
4288 X 2848
8.60 MB
240 PPI

| | |
|---|---|
| FILE NAME | ogroveJEH_2716.jpg |
| DOCUMENT TYPE | JPEG |
| APPLICATION | Adobe Photoshop CS4 |
| DATE CREATED | 4/26/07. 11:03:50 AM |
| FILE SIZE | 8.60 MB |
| DIMENSIONS | 4288 x 2848 |
| IN INCHES | 17.9″ x 11.9″ |
| RESOLUTION | 240 ppi |
| BIT DEPTH | 8 |
| COLOR MODE | RGB |
| COLOR PROFILE | Adobe RGB (1998) |
| EXPOSURE MODE | Manual |
| FOCAL LENGTH | 19.0 mm |
| IN 35 MM FILM | 119.0 mm |
| LENS | 7.0 x 35.0 mm |
| MAX APERTURE | 2.8 |
| CUSTOM RENDERED | Normal |
| WHITE BALANCE | Auto |
| DIGITAL ZOOM RATIO | 100 % |
| SCENE CAPTURE | Standard |
| GAIN CONTROL | 0 |
| CONTRAST | 1 |
| SATURATION | 0 |
| SHARPNESS | Normal |
| SENSING MODE | One-chip sensor |
| FILE SOURCE | Digital camera |
| MAKE | Nikon Corporation |
| MODEL | Nikon D3 |
| SERIAL NUMBER | 5049838 |
| CREATOR | Jill Heinerth |
| ADDRESS | 5989 NE County Road |
| STATE | Florida |
| WEB SITE | www.IntoThePlanet.com |

file is generally not compatible with the publishing industry, but these files can be easily saved as a TIFF or JPEG after processing.

If RAW is available, it is the best choice for photographers that care about image quality. Allowing your camera to process your image in any way, means that it is throwing away data. To utilize all that RAW files have to offer, a program like Photoshop is almost a necessity.

Most cameras permit the photographer to change formats on the fly. When you take family snapshots at your friend's wedding, switch to lower resolution JPEGs that can be quickly viewed and shared. But don't forget to switch the camera back to high-res TIFF or RAW before your next dive trip. You might not get another chance to photograph a whale shark, and you'll want the highest quality image of your amazing underwater encounter!

## Metadata and EXIF

Digital cameras embed information about how a photo was shot into an extension of the photographic file. This information is called EXIF, which stands for Exchangeable Image File Format. EXIF records information about camera settings when the image was shot. It documents shutter speed, aperture, strobe settings, film speed (ISO), exposure compensation (EV), camera mode (automatic, aperture priority, etc.), orientation, date, time, picture thumbnail and other details specific to your camera.

This information is very valuable when you want to review your successes and failures from a shoot. It is like having a photo assistant taking continuous notes on each shot. This information can also be enhanced in programs like Photoshop, Bridge, Lightroom and Aperture. Keywords, locations and other data may be added and then made "searchable" within a website or on the Internet. Your copyright may also be appended to the file.

It is important to correctly set the time and date within your camera, because this information becomes part of the EXIF data. If you need to search for photos later and can recall a rough date, you will be able to track the file within your computer. Some photographers have even linked their GPS data to their EXIF data. Since GPS devices can monitor your location related to date and time, these data points can be merged in simple software resulting in a precise GPS location for each photo. This information can be further linked to programs like Google Earth so that someone searching a particular location on earth can link to your photos.

If you want to be able to search and sell your photography as stock, it is worthwhile to immediately invest a little time to generate notes about your photos in EXIF and add your copyright information to protect your assets.

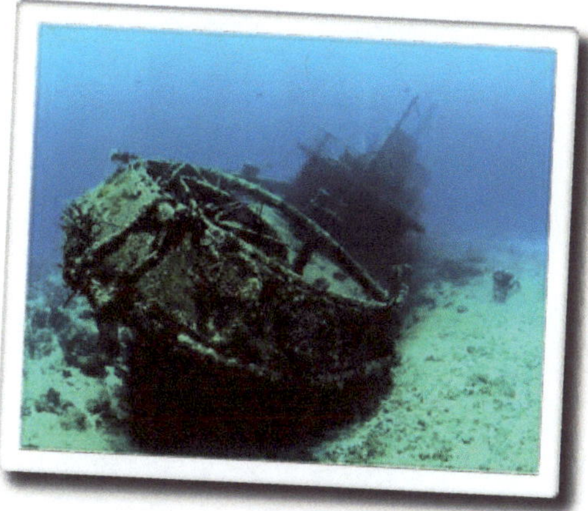

High resolution image (above) and low resolution image showing pixelation (below).

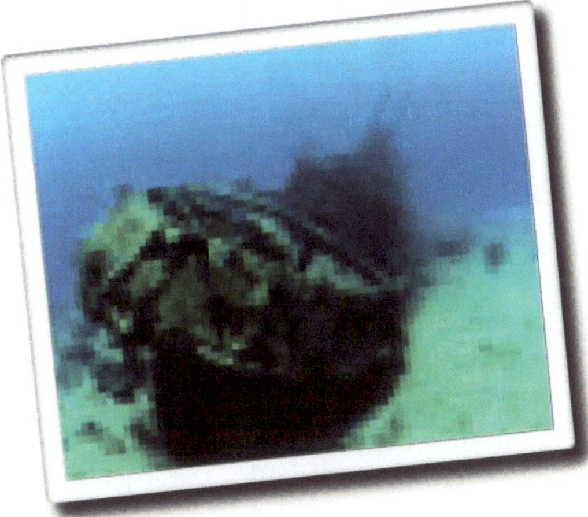

## Resolution

When you take a picture with a digital camera, the light strikes a digital sensor array, instead of film stock. These arrays are computer chips made up of tiny sensors called "pixels." The more pixels on the sensor array, the higher the resolution of the photograph.

Pixels are laid out in rows and columns on the chip. For instance, a sensor array might have 3000 pixels laid out horizontally and 2000 pixels laid out vertically. If you multiply the horizontal resolution by the vertical resolution, you will be calculating the "megapixel" rating of the camera. This sensor, would therefore belong to a camera capable of shooting 6 million pixels, otherwise know as a 6 megapixel camera.

Higher "megapixel-rated" cameras not only shoot higher resolution photos, but they also allow for much bigger enlargements without loss of quality.

When light strikes the image sensor, individual pixels become energized. A series of electronic color and image filters convert information into electronic data. This data is organized and compressed so that it can be efficiently stored in a temporary buffer and then moved onto a memory card as a digital signal.

If a camera has a large buffer, then many photographs can be taken in quick succession. Less expensive cameras have smaller buffers, that mean you will have to wait before you can shoot and store your next photo.

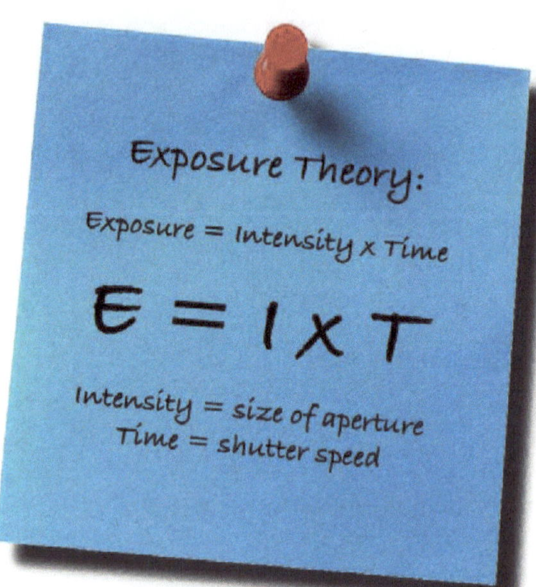


## The Theory of Exposure

In the earliest days of image making, photographers used a device called a "pinhole camera." This was simply a small box containing a roll or plate of light sensitive material or film. A tiny hole in the front of the box could be opened to allow light to strike the surface of the material. Larger holes allowed more light in, and therefore a brighter exposure. When the hole was held open for a long duration, it gave time for more light to strike the film plane. The actual image exposure was a relationship of light intensity and time. The intensity of the light was controlled by the size of the pinhole and the time was controlled by the duration that the shutter curtain was held open.

Modern photographers express this relationship with an equation that forms the pivotal theory for all photography:

**E = I x T**

**Exposure = Intensity x Time**

The modern "pinhole" is called the aperture. This opening, that allows light into the camera, controls the intensity of the light striking the sensor. It has also been referred to as an iris since the opening works much like that of the human eye. Aperture openings are expressed as "f-stops."

Time is controlled by shutter speed, which can be selected in seconds or fractions of seconds.

## Aperture Control

Apertures or f-stops are expressed in sizes. A small f-stop number like f/2.8 represents a large opening, allowing access to high intensity light. A large f-number such as f/22 is a very small opening that admits a tiny amount of light. Older cameras had a limited number of f-stops that could be dialed in with a manual knob. Each stepped opening was either half or double the amount of light as the previous stop. Therefore, f/2.8 was twice as much light as f/5.6. Similarly, f/22 permitted half as much light as f/16. Many digital cameras have almost infinite selections of f-stops available when using either Manual Control settings or Aperture Control settings. However, like most modern camera controls, these settings are derived from historical cameras. Understanding the history behind the design of older cameras, helps the photographer master control over newer digital models.

When you buy a lens, one of the product specifications describes the limits of the aperture. A lens that can open up to a large aperture of f/2.8, f/1.8 or even larger is known as a "fast lens." Most lens will all close down to f/22 or f/32. A full stop difference on the specifications will indicate that the lens may be capable of requiring only half the light to illuminate a photo. That's why fast lenses are generally more expensive and usually a good selection for low light conditions like underwater photography.

## Controlling Time

Shutter Speed is expressed in increments of seconds such as 1/125th of a second, 1/500th of a second or 1 second. Light strikes the film or image sensor for this duration. An additional increment called "Bulb" or "B" leaves the shutter open while the shutter button is depressed or alternatively, opens the shutter on the first button press and closes it on the second depression. Some remote controls can also be used to open and close the camera shutter allowing for long exposures.

In general, fast shutter speeds like 1/500, 1/1000 and higher will "freeze" the action. Sports photographers looking to capture the moment of a dunk shot will use fast shutter speeds. Similarly, nature photographers trying to capture a distant bird alighting on a tree will use fast shutter speeds for sharp, stop-action shots.

Slow shutter speeds blur action, but they also allow maximum light penetration in dark environments. Most photographers can only effectively handhold shutter speeds of 1/60 or faster. Slower speeds like 1/15 result in blurring from camera shake. However, if the camera is stabilized, or mounted on a tripod, then slower shutter speeds will yield acceptable focus.

## Equivalent Exposure

Modern cameras have several programmable options beyond fully automatic control, yet many photographers never use these tools. Aperture Priority, Shutter Priority and Manual settings give photographers the chance to master control over the camera and obtain truly artistic results. Understanding how the camera thinks is the key to originality.

You are smarter than your camera!

## Film Speed

There is one more element that empowers us to control the exposure equation and that is an often misunderstood specification called the ISO number or ASA. These numbers, used to indicate the speed, or sensitivity of a certain film stock, are in fact acronyms for International Standards Organization and American Standards Association. These organizations created light sensitivity standards for photographic film that helped us to de-

### Equivalent Exposures

The table below illustrates several equivalent exposures. Adjusting one entire f-stop is equivalent to one entire shutter speed. Adjusting one entire shutter speed is equivalent to one entire f-stop. 1/125th @ f/11 is the same exposure as 1/60th @ f/16, yet selecting one or the other offers up different visual results that will be further described under the heading, Depth of Field.

| F-STOP | APERTURE |
|---|---|
| f 2.8 | 1/2000 |
| f 5.6 | 1/1000 |
| f 8 | 1/500 |
| f 11 | 1/250 |
| F 16 | 1/125 |
| f 22 | 1/60 |

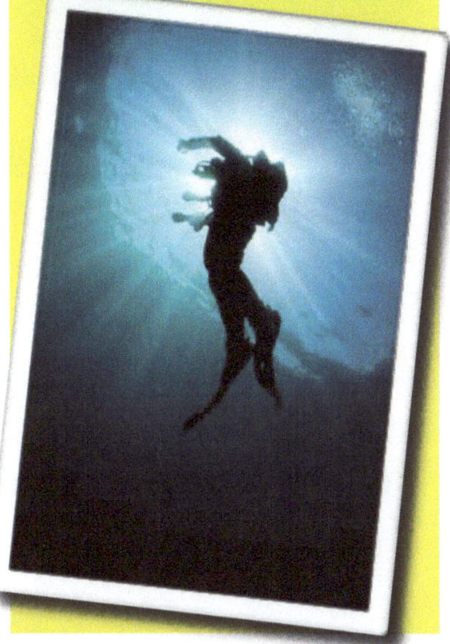

## ISO Range

SLOW FILM SPEED
ISO 100
less sensitive to light
greater detail
fine focus
less grain or noise
great for macro

ISO 200

ISO 400

ISO 800

FAST FILM SPEED
ISO 1600
more sensitive to light
less detail
softer focus
more grain or noise
can shoot in low light
best to stop action

termine equivalency between different brands. A low ISO number like 25 indicated a slow film or one that needed more light to make an exposure. ISO 25 film is a good choice for studio work where there is abundant light available. A high ISO film like 1600 is very sensitive to light and would be a good choice to capture fast action. Sports photographers might always load 1600 ISO, but someone shooting nature close-ups would prefer 25 ISO. Although the 1600 ISO film would freeze action well, it tended to be grainier than a slow film. Traditional film stock contained a light sensitive emulsion known as silver halide. The larger the size of each grain of silver, the more sensitive to light is was. As the image was enlarged, the grain became more visible. Even though we now use a sensor instead of film, the same rules apply. A slow film speed will net the richest, most saturated color with the least amount of grain. We now refer to the relative graininess of digital sensors as "noise."

Ultimately you can disregard shutter speed, aperture and ISO controls on your camera and select an automatic control that will make these choices for you. However, gaining mastery over these selections is what will make your photography unique and creative.

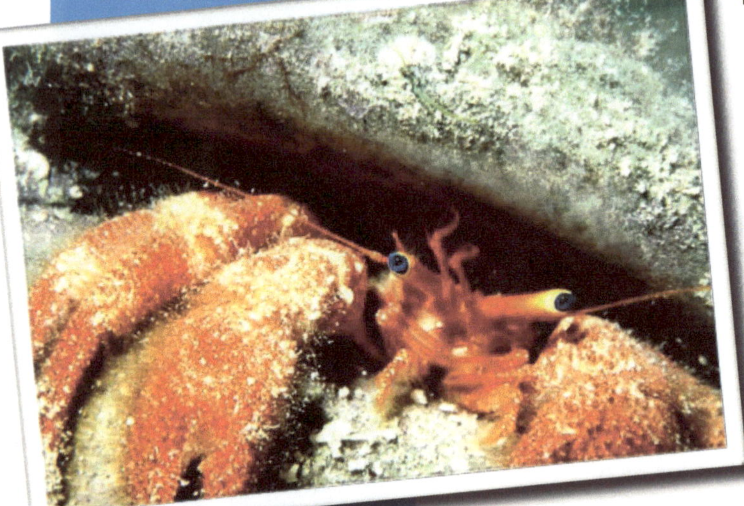

Macro shots are best taken with a slow film speed to enhance color saturation and detail

## Depth of Field

Depth of Field is the zone of the photograph that appears to be in sharp focus. It extends approximately one-third the distance in front of and two-thirds the distance behind the subject on which you are focussed. Depth of field increases when you "stop-down" (use a smaller aperture) to create your exposure. Depth of field is controlled by the aperture, or f-stop. Large apertures such as f/2.8, f/4 and f/5.6 will minimize depth of field or narrow the range of focus in a picture. Smaller apertures like f/16, f/22 and f/32 will allow for a greater range of focus or more depth of field.

Although equivalent exposures represent mathematically comparable amounts of light entering the camera, they will result in different looking photographs. One exposure may be optimal, but others may yield greater depth of field, special motion effects or the ability to stop action.

## Depth of Field / Equivalent Exposures

| F-STOP | SHUTTER SPEED | ADVANTAGES/ DISADVANTAGES |
|---|---|---|
| f 2.8 | 1/2000 | Freezes action least depth of field |
| f 4 | 1/1000 | |
| f 5.6 | 1/500 | |
| f 8 | 1/250 | |
| f 11 | 1/125 | |
| f 16 | 1/60 | |
| f 22 | 1/30 | Best depth of field least motion blur |

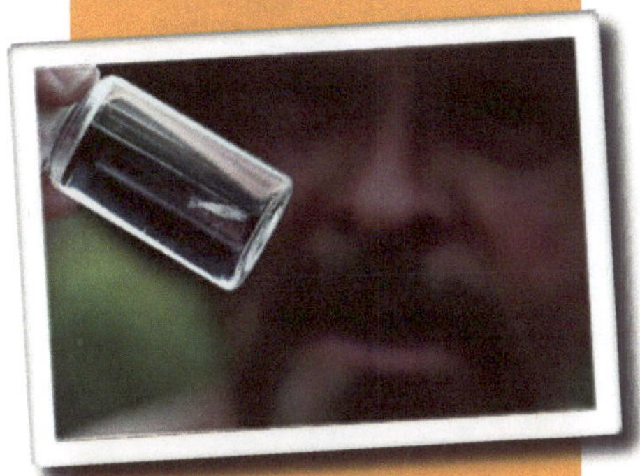

A narrow depth of field is used to highlight the sample collected by the scientist.

When looking through your DSLR viewfinder, you will not see the results of your camera settings and choices in exposure. Cameras focus with an open shutter and aperture, thus allowing maximal light to compose and focus a shot. After depressing the shutter button, you can review the results of your choices on the LCD display.

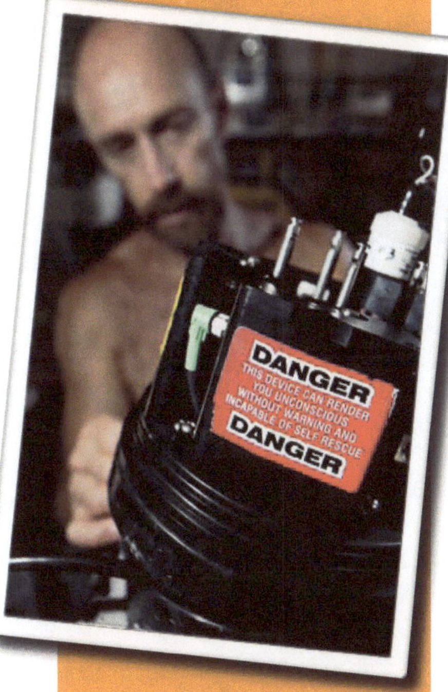


Narrow depth of field is used to highlight the rebreather's "Danger" label and de-emphasize the diver preparing the equipment

Many people carefully manage aperture settings to control depth of field in their photos. This is called Aperture Priority. With Aperture Priority, the photographer selects the desired f-stop and the camera will choose the best corresponding shutter speed. By selecting a small aperture like f/22, depth of field increases, but will require a longer shutter speed to achieve the best exposure. If you shoot a crowd of people at f/22, they may all be in focus. Yet, if the photographer selects a large aperture such as f/2.8,

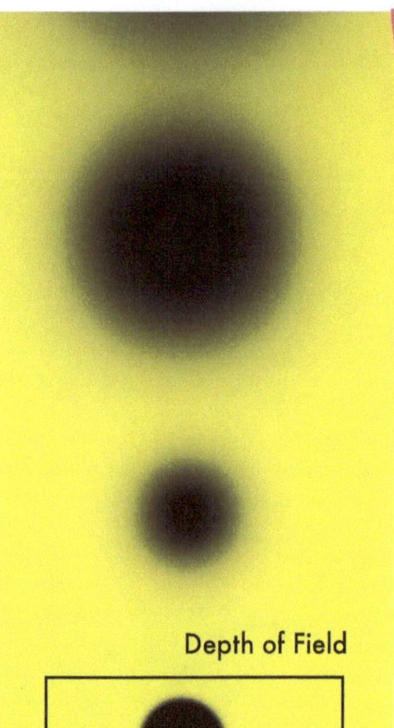

Depth of Field

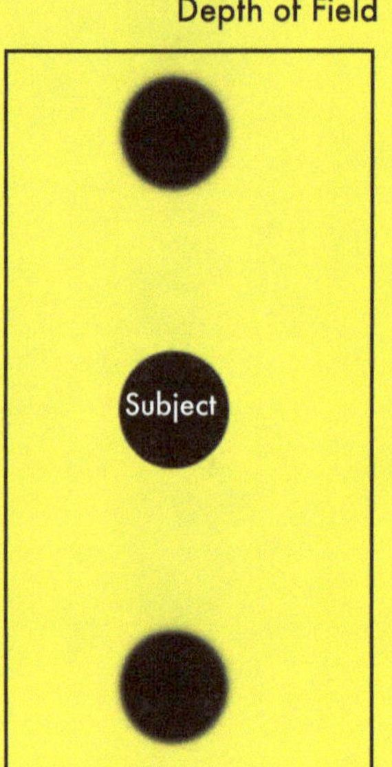


**Depth of Field:**
Is the distance from the nearest point of acceptably sharp focus to the farthest acceptably sharp point of acceptably sharp focus of the scene being photographed. A narrow depth of field is a small plane of acceptable focus in a scene.

with a corresponding fast shutter speed, the depth of field decreases, and they may highlight one sharp person in a soft focus crowd.

The newest cameras offer preprogrammed selections like portrait, landscape, backlit or even night photography mode. Your camera manual will describe these settings fully, but be aware, these settings will usually apply unique depth of field effects. A portrait setting may offer a narrow depth of field, while landscape will offer greater. A night setting may open the aperture wide, sacrificing depth of field.

Understanding depth of field may be difficult at first, but if you experiment with different f-stops while shooting the same scene, it becomes very apparent.

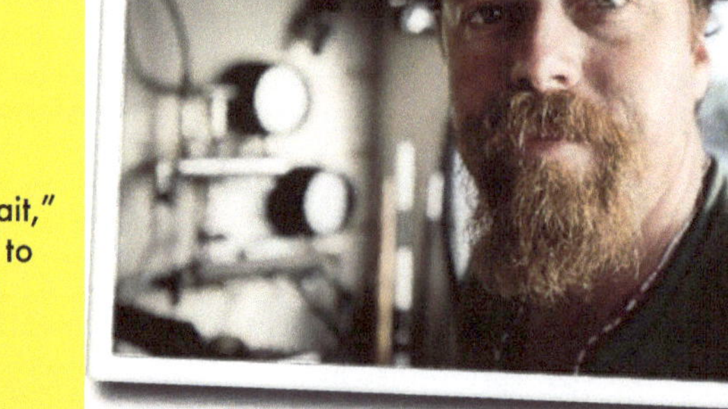

In an "environmental portrait," depth of field is often used to accentuate the subject and bring subtlety to his or her surroundings.

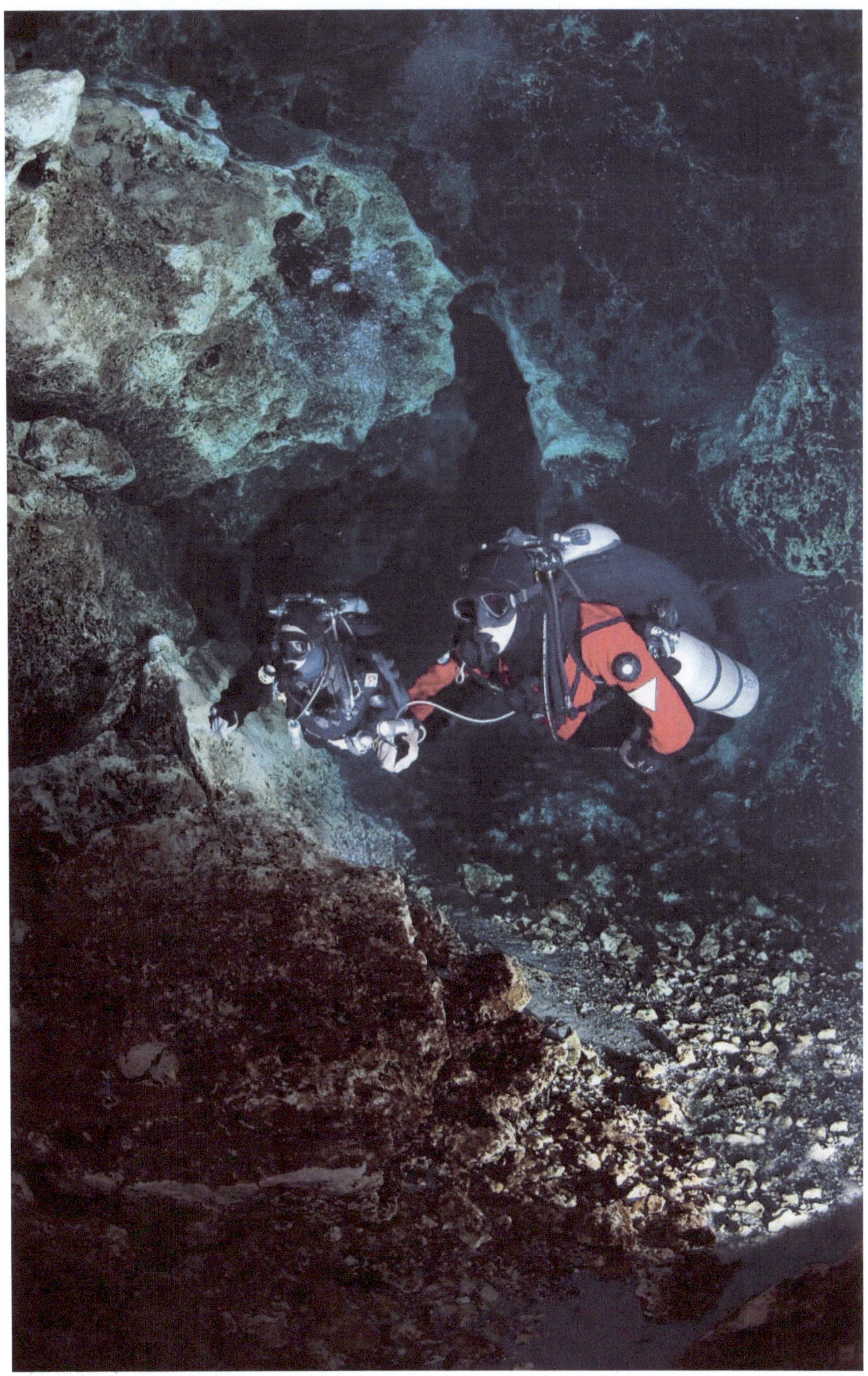

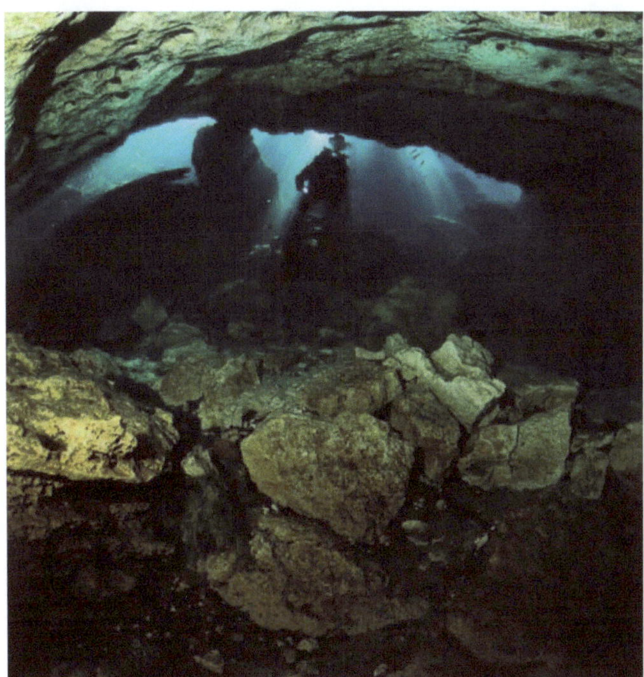

## Light Loss in Water

The underwater environment presents additional, unique photographic issues. Beyond equipment, skill and safety issues, the water itself is a challenging medium for the photographer.

When sunlight hits the surface of the water, much of it is reflected back skyward. Very little light actually penetrates the surface to illuminate the depths. When the sun is almost directly overhead, the maximum amount of light penetrates the underwater environment. Many people prefer to take photographs between 10 am and 2 pm for this reason alone. At other times of day, sunlight strikes the surface of the water, reflecting back a greater majority of light. During these off hours, less light will penetrate, but it may reach your subject with a more intriguing angle and color.

Shooting from below, in an upward direction, will separate the subject from the darker water of the depths.

## Thinking About Light

Before you swim off into the interior of a wreck or a cave, you must first learn to shoot well in open water diving scenarios. Thinking about, and looking at light, is a critical aspect of every photograph.

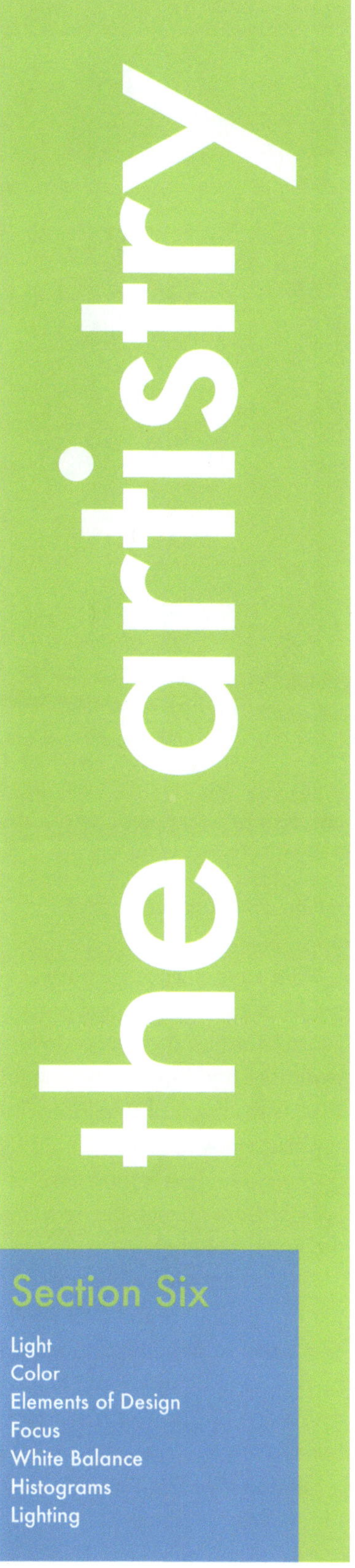

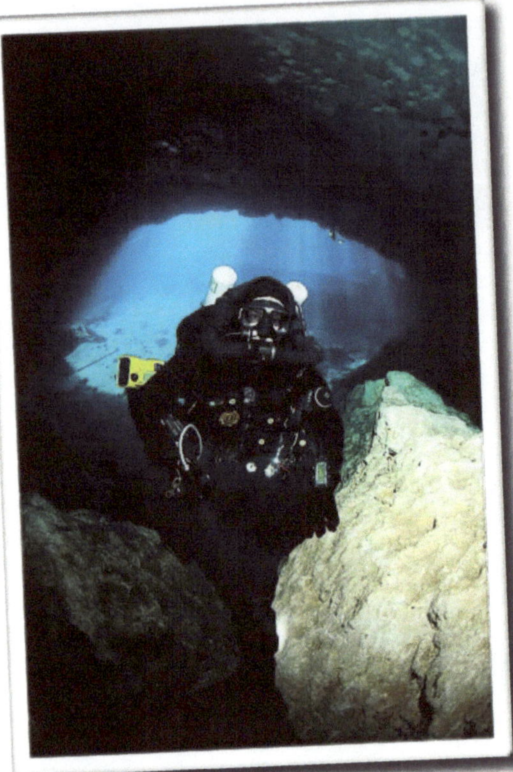

This exposure has been carefully balanced. In order to emphasize the background light, the aperture is wide open and the shutter speed is maximized to 1/60 second. The diver is highlighted with a soft fill from a low power setting on the strobes.

The cavern zone or doorway of a wreck is one the prettiest places to shoot. Learn to see and appreciate what light is available and figure out how to control it. Take advantage of available light and then supplement with justified light (light that appears to come from a diver's hand-held light or from the sun penetrating through the water column).

A camera strobe is capable of filling the foreground areas with light, but you also need to plan the exposure so that the background filtering light illuminates the rest of the photo. This is called balancing the exposure.

Imagine yourself in a completely dark room. When someone throws open the exterior door, it takes a moment for your eyes to adjust and see the green lawn outside the door. There is such a high contrast between the bright, outside light and environment that you are standing in, that it may be impossible to register the details of the interior of the door-frame, while still seeing the details of the green lawn. If someone turns on an interior light, both may appear better balanced.

As a photographer you can make creative choices. Do you want the silhouette of a black door-frame, with a beautiful green lawn? Do you want the details of the interior of the door with a glaring bright white light pouring in? Do you want to balance both? This is where the creativity in photography starts.

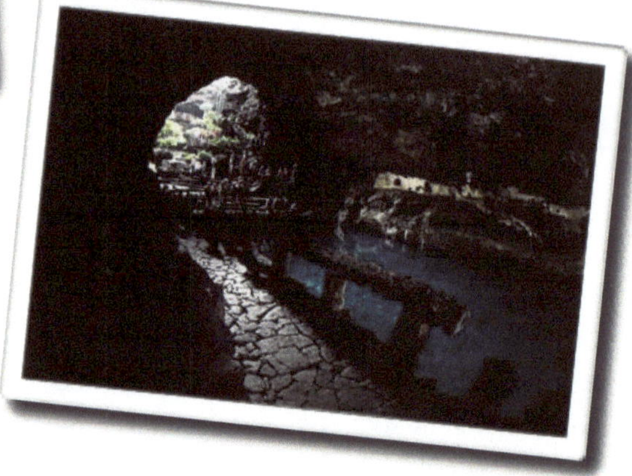

The exposure above is balanced, while the photograph below shows what happens when the background is over-exposed.

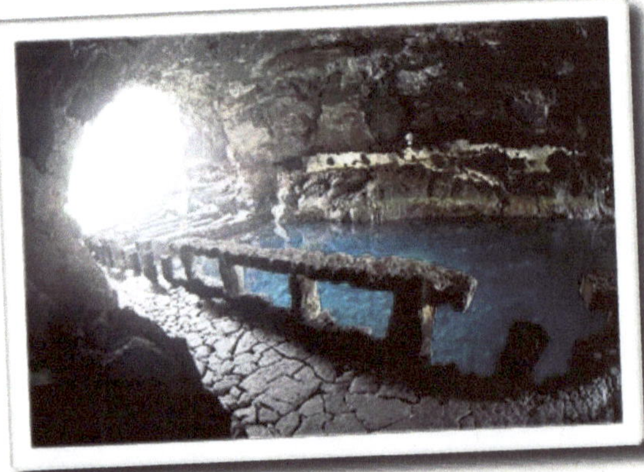

## Color Loss

Water acts like a giant filter, removing colors as you descend. The red end of the spectrum is absorbed rather quickly in as little as 15 feet of water. The deeper you go, the more you arrive in a blue/green world, almost void of warm colors. Even in clear water, at depths of 100 feet, there is very little light penetrating through the water column and very little color left other than indigo and blue.

To compensate for color and light loss, divers often carry handheld lights to restore the beauty of the natural world. Few diver-carried lights will be bright enough to illuminate a photograph. Instead, camera strobes are used to artificially provide the natural light and color of the landscape. Color is lost vertically in the water column but also horizontally when more filtering water is in between the camera and subject. Depending on the power of the strobe, it may only be able to properly illuminate things that are close to the light source. More powerful units may have a greater ability to throw and direct light.

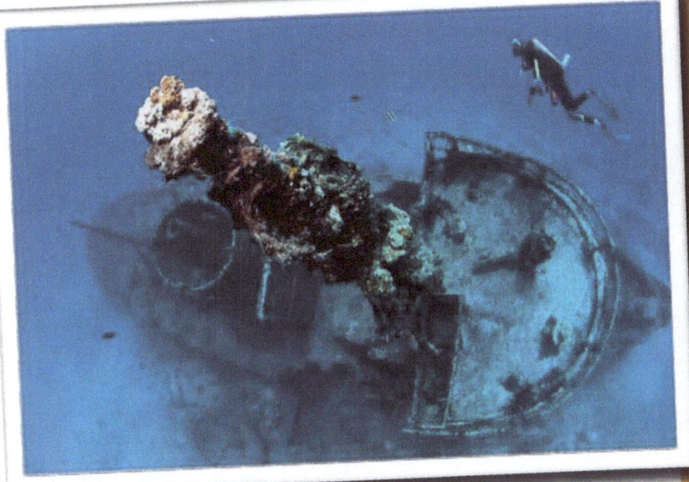

### Color Spectrum

As depth increases, the warm end of the color spectrum is lost first. Reds disappear, followed by oranges, yellows and greens until only blue, indigo and violet remain. A strobe will restore the natural colors in your photos.

A strobe is only capable of throwing light for a short distance to bring out the colors normally filtered by the water column. At greater distances, filtration reduces the color spectrum to a blue-green monochromatic world.

## Composition

Composition is the artistry in photography and it refers to how elements are arranged within a frame. As such, composition can be very subjective. What is beautiful to one, may not be as pleasing to another viewer. Even with the subjective realities of art appreciation, there are some general rules that will aid a diver in creating beautiful compositions.

There are seven basic elements of composition that are pleasing to the human eye. They are described below.

## Path

The human eye needs to be able to move around the frame of the photograph. Visual elements that point the viewer's attention around the frame are pleasing. A diver looking at a fish in profile allows the viewer's eye to dance from the diver to the fish and back within the frame. A fish swimming away from the camera, confers a disturbing feeling of retreat.

The subject in motion needs room to move within the frame. If they are in the corner of the picture swimming off the edge of the photo, it will leave the viewer feeling disjointed.

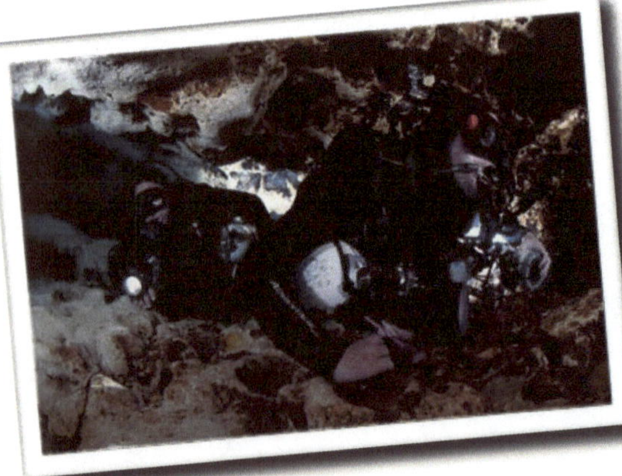

The diver's position (above) evokes motion and action, giving a pleasing path or line of travel in the composition. The rope (below) creates leading lines the carry the viewer through the visual elements of the photo.

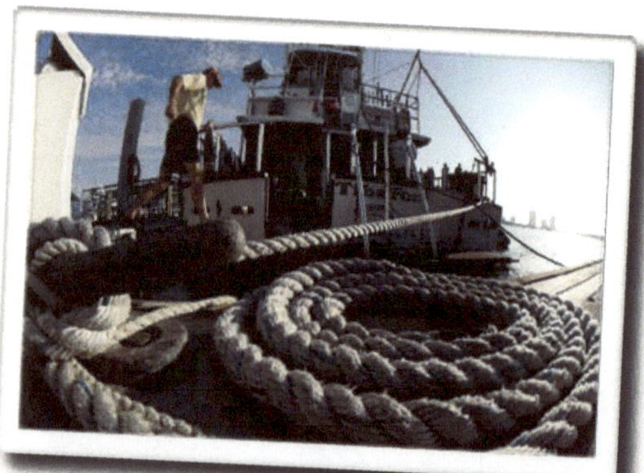

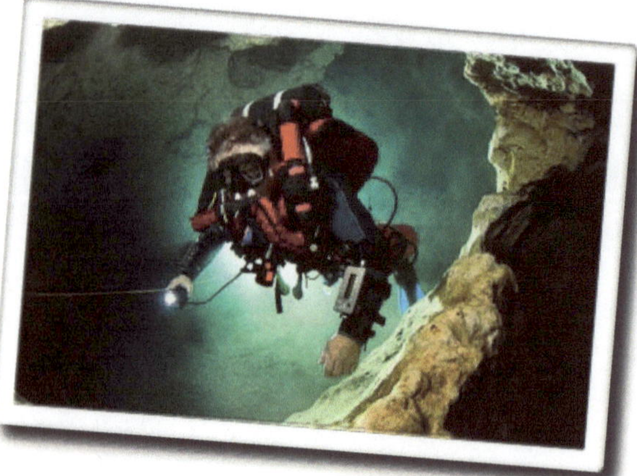

A model posed in slight profile is preferred over a head-on shot. Within the composition, there is room for the diver to move through the frame of reference.

## Shape

Geometric and organic shapes are created in a photograph by the arrangement of objects. Sometimes they can have unintended consequences on the photo. When shooting a diver head-on, sometimes their fins appear as though they are coming out of their head. This posture may represent good diving technique that prevents the fins from contact with the reef, but the appearance of this posture makes the diver look like they have Mickey-Mouse ears. If the model is asked to rotate their position to a slight profile, the resulting line and shape may create a beautiful diagonal leading line through the picture.

## Color

Color is often associated with different moods. Soft muted colors may evoke peacefulness, where boldly contrasted colors may be considered brash. Colors that oppose each other on the color wheel tend to be very pleasing.

Black and white photographs have their own special allure. With access to modern editing equipment, it is always better to shoot in full color and then translate the photo to black and white during post-processing. Black and white is excellent for vintage subjects like shipwrecks, and duotones are also very pleasing. In this case, black and white photos are tinted with a second ink color like blue or sepia, adding even more depth and a historic feeling to the subject.

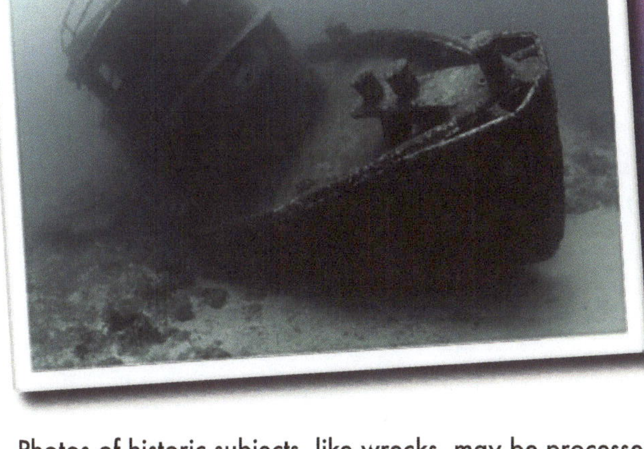

Photos of historic subjects, like wrecks, may be processed in black and white or as a duotone. This treatment also helps the diver get around milky water conditions.

### Texture

The patterns on a surface create may be used to evoke tactile sensations. Orderly patterns found in the undersea world, like coral polyps or sea fans, may give a pleasing sense of order to a shot.

## The Color Wheel

Colors that are opposite to each other on the color wheel are pleasing combinations. Reds and yellows stand out vibrantly in blue water conditions. Under-lit shots appear drab (bottom).

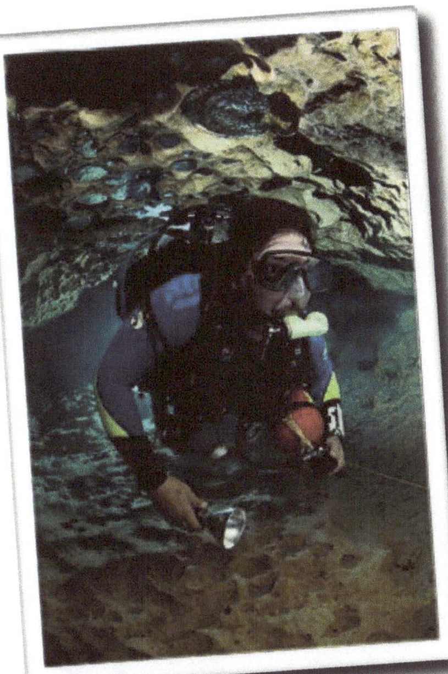

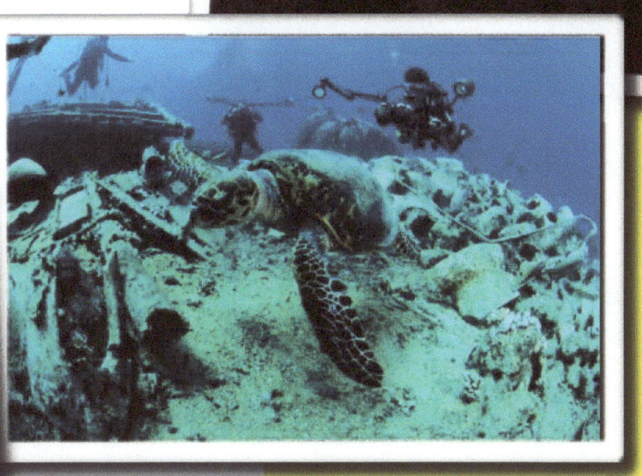

### Size

The relative size of one object to another can give a very different result. A large foreground shark with a tiny diver in the background, will make the viewer uneasy about the safety of a diver. The reverse shot of a large foreground diver viewing a smaller background shark will give a completely different feel.

### Perspective

Perspective is the illusion of depth. A photograph with a discernible foreground, middle and background will appear to be deep and will naturally draw the viewer's interest.

### Space

Some objects appear as positive items in a photo and the empty area in between is perceived as negative space. The balance between negative and positive space will affect how the viewer feels about a photo.

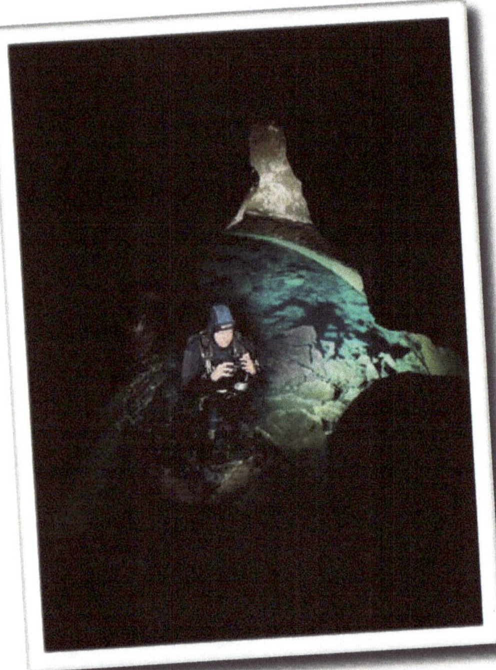

Negative space can create an imposing feeling of weight and can focus the viewer on a particular subject.

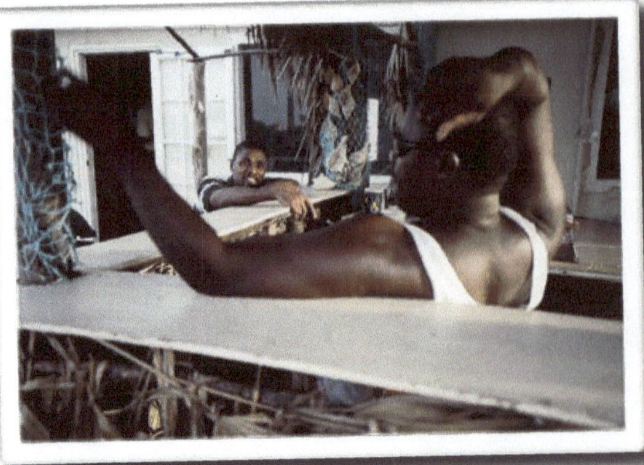

Using a combination of depth of field, size and perspective, the composition gives the viewer the impression that they are being allowed in to an intimate conversation.

## Artistry

The artistry and unique aspects of a photograph are created by experimenting with the seven elements of design. The right combination can create a harmonious, pleasing image that may be judged as beautiful. A different combination could result in a photograph that is deemed disturbing or jarring. Even with excellent exposure, a diver whose head is cut off the edge of the photo will not win any awards.

When using a model, the photographer has the opportunity to select how the viewer should interact with the diver. If the camera viewpoint looks straight down on a diver in a bait ball with sharks, he may seem vulnerable. If the angle of the photo looks up at the diver who fills the frame while he feeds the sharks, this may leave more of an impression of power and control.

## Rule of Thirds

The Rule of Thirds is an ancient design concept followed by most visual artists. If you take the frame of reference and divide it into three columns and three rows, you will have a photo that is divided into nine boxes. The Rule of Thirds teaches us that the points of the intersecting lines are the most interesting to the human brain. The general composition should be grouped into elements that fall into the thirds, but the action or point of interest should take place on the intersections with the motion occurring "into" the frame, rather than "out" of the frame.

Almost everything in our natural world falls into this pattern of design. Whether it is star nebula or chambered Nautilus shell, these elegantly designed works of nature fall into the Rule of Thirds. As such, it is believed, that the human mind finds peace and pleasure in things that follow the golden rules of composition in the natural world.

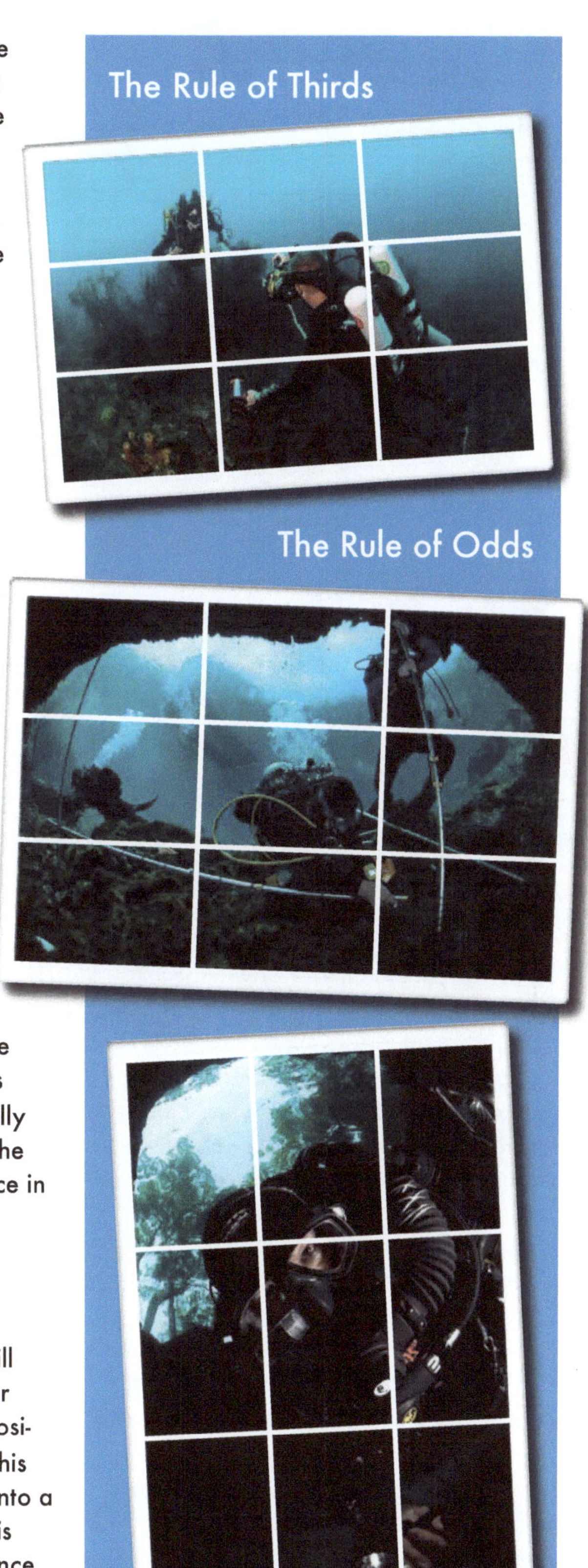


## The Rule of Odds

This rule suggests that an odd number of subjects in a shot is more pleasing than an even number of items. This stems from the organization of the Rule of Thirds. Thus, if you have more than one diver in a shot, it will be more pleasing to see three, rather than two. In this light, triangles are also pleasing negative or positive spaces within a shot. The human face is essentially an equilateral triangle from the eyes to the mouth. As a result, our minds find balance in that shape.

## Depth of Field

Limiting the focal range in a photo will bring attention to the object in focus. Our eyes are naturally attracted to the compositional element that is in sharpest focus. This technique can be used to draw the eye into a particular item or quadrant of a shot. This simplification makes the viewing experience "easy" and therefore pleasurable.

## Getting a Sharp Shot

Getting clear, crisp images underwater is very reliant on shutter speed. You may need a slow shutter speed to maximize the light reaching the image sensor, but anything slower than 1/60th second is difficult to hold steady underwater. Faster shutter speeds may be necessary to get a crisp image. Shutter speeds of 1/125 or faster have an added bonus of capturing and freezing beams of light cascading from above a cavern, reef or wreck opening.

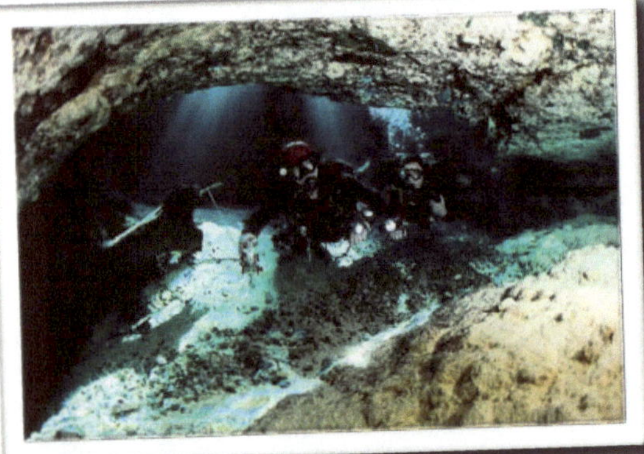

Focusing through an underwater viewfinder has its own unique challenges. You'll want to buy as large a viewfinder as you can get with a large LCD screen for review. Using a "hood" or a magnifier, such as Aquatica's Aquaview, to exclude light reflection around the viewfinder also helps. Using a mask with a black silicone skirt will help to eliminate distracting light reflections.

Since you will be viewing menus and functions on the LCD screen, you may also discover that you need an optical magnifier, or gauge reader placed in your mask to read the smallest text. Be careful to glue the optical magnifier in a location that won't interfere with your ability to focus, since the magnifier can be distracting if poorly placed.

Good buoyancy control and a steady hand will also aid in getting a photo that is free of motion blur.

Less capable cameras may have a slight delay time between depressing the shutter and actually firing a shot. This delay is known as shutter lag or lag time. A photographer may find it useful to carefully achieve neutral buoyancy, exhale and then move forward while slowly inhaling in order capture a flighty fish shot. Resist the urge to hold your breath, but try to time your approach to lessen bubbles that could scare wildlife as you move in close. It's a delicate dance that will improve as you practice.

## Examining Your Shots

### Histograms

When I first transitioned to digital photography, I was disappointed that photos shot underwater in the cave looked excellent on the screen, but were terribly underexposed when downloaded to my computer. The LCD screen can lure you into thinking you have a great shot, especially when viewed in low-light conditions. With a good understanding of a feature called histograms, you will get a much higher percentage of well-exposed photographs.

The histogram is actually a metering function of the camera which is viewed on the LCD screen after the image is shot. As a matter of practice, the LCD photo image should only be used to evaluate composition, whereas the histogram should be used to critique exposure.

One of the considerations of exposure is contrast, or the range of tones between the lightest and darkest areas of a photograph. Many people are familiar with contrast controls on television and computer screens.

Traditional photographic film could only provide an acceptable exposure in the range of a few f-stops. Today's digital camera sensors can record a larger range of acceptable light, considered to be around five or six f-stops. Still, some high contrast underwater photographs may contain a range of 10 or 12 f-stops of light.

**How to Read Histograms**

A histogram is a bar graph that shows you 256 brightness levels for your image from pure black on the left to pure white on the right. It also allows you to see the distribution of tones in an image. The taller the peak of a bar on the graph, the more of that particular color, you will see in the photo. The more pixels on the right, the brighter the image. The more pixels on the left, the darker the image. An underexposed photo will show all the pixels piled on the left and an overexposed photo will show all the pixels piled on the right. A flat looking photo will have all the pixels bunched in the middle. A contrasty photo will have tall peaks on each end of the histogram.

When we review a histogram, we concentrate mainly on the far left and far right. If bars fill up the left of the screen and peak at the top, then critical information has been lost. You cannot lighten the darkest area to recover detail if the histogram peaks on the left. The converse is true on the right side. If the bars fill up the right side and peak at the top, then there are areas of complete whiteness without any detail remaining. When the right or left side of the histogram is filled to the top of the graph, we call this "clipping."

Well-distributed peaks and valleys allow for a lot of adjustment in image editing programs, although a histogram does not need to cover an entire window. An underwater cave image should not clip on the left, but most of the data will still fill the

Normal Histogram

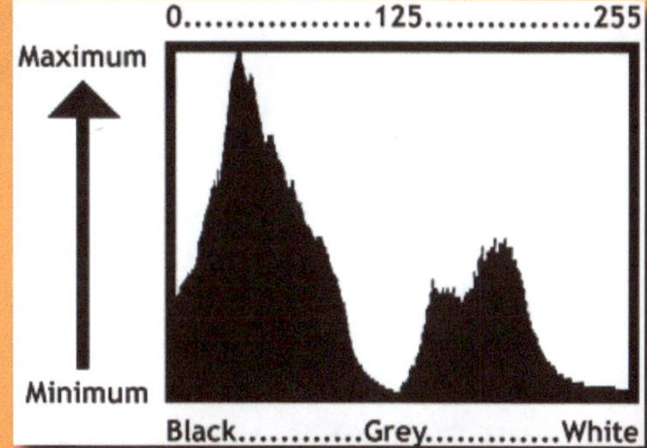


Overexposed Histogram

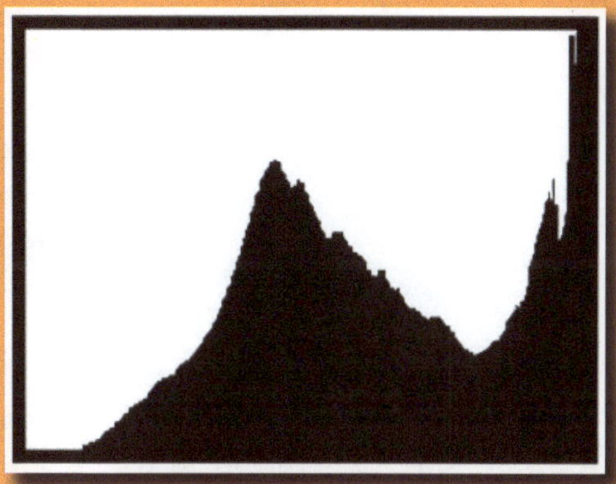

Underexposed Histogram

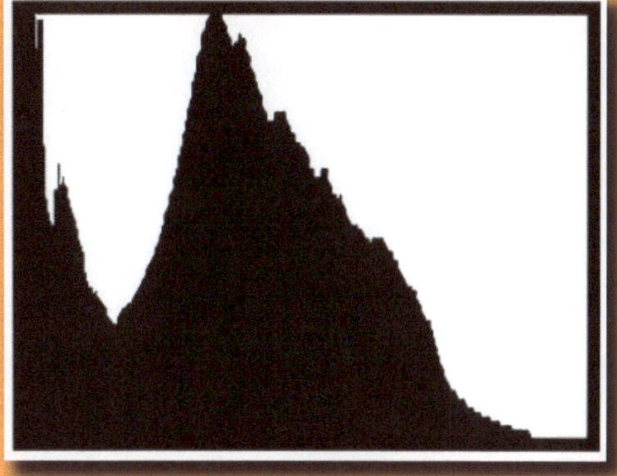

Your camera may show a master histogram and perhaps additional color histograms. The master will be most useful to review.

## White Balance

| | |
|---|---|
| 1800° K | candlelight<br>more orange<br>warm |
| 2800° K | standard<br>lightbulb |
| 5500° K | bright sun<br>HID lights |
| 6000° K | strobes |
| 6500° K | cloudy day |
| 8000° K | hazy day<br>more blue<br>cool |

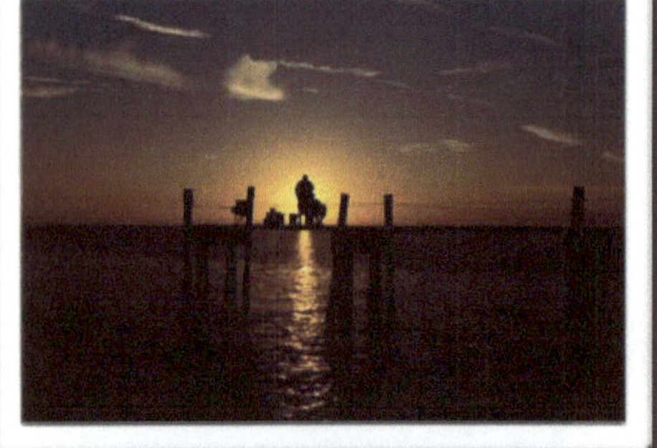

This photo shows the natural white balance, as shot.

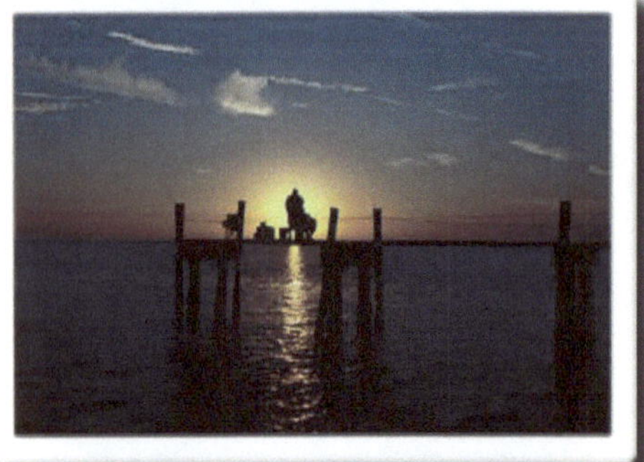

This photo shows the camera white balance set on "auto."

left side of the bar graph since this dark blue environment does not contain all the colors of the spectrum.

### Using Histograms Underwater to Make Adjustments

Many digital cameras offer several viewing options on the LCD screen. The full frame screen is a good tool for composition and a reasonable judge for serious focusing errors. The "highlight" screen, available on some cameras, will flicker the area where white has been clipped from the image. The human eye is not very forgiving to an image with blown-out white areas or highlights, but understands better, an image with dark, clipped shadow areas. We call dark photos artistic and moody but clipped highlights are considered overexposed mistakes. Refer to the histogram screen after your shot and quickly scan it for clipping on either end. Exposure and composition adjustments can then be made to improve the next shot.

Exposure adjustments can be made in several ways. In manual mode, the f-stop or shutter speed can be adjusted. Light can also be added or subtracted using the camera's exposure compensation button (EV +/-). So, even if you have chosen to shoot using automatic modes, you should tweak the settings after reviewing the histogram. Once you have mastered using histograms, you can use them to create a very unique "look" for your photos and return from every dive with well-exposed shots that can be improved in image-editing programs.

## White Balance

For those that are completely new to digital imaging, white balance will be a new concept. White balance is a function on a digital camera that compensates for different colors of light that are being emitted by different light sources. These light sources can be sunlight, diving lights, and camera strobes. Water filters light in different ways, creating a variety of colors. Various depths filter natural light to give unique coloration. White balancing a camera compensates for those differences.

With film cameras, we used to select film stock and filters for different lighting conditions. Fluorescent lighting warranted a different film selection than outdoor photography. We also used filters to adjust different film types for the "color temperature" of the light.

Color temperature is measured in Kelvin degrees (K). A common light bulb in your house might emit 2800K, where mid-day sun may average 5500K. Modern HID primary diving lights appear blue because they have high color temperature bulbs, where older incandescent lights appear more orange with lower color temperatures.

With digital cameras, we don't need to select different film or filters, but we do need to adjust white balance for the conditions of a given day, dive and even depth.

White balance is not a measure of brightness, but rather a measure of the relative color of an object in different scenarios as seen in the chart on the previous sidebar.

### How does White Balance Work?

When we white balance, we teach the camera what white looks like on a particular day and condition. Once the camera makes white look truly white, then every other color will look accurate under the same light sources. White balance can also be used to deliberately alter a photographic palette and introduce creative color-casts for special effects.

Digital cameras may have more than one technique for selecting white balance. Some cameras have an automatic feature that continuously re-samples for white balance. Some cameras allow the photographer to pre-program different white balances for different looks. High-end cameras will also allow the photographer to select a color temperature on the Kelvin temperature scale.

To manually select white balance, the photographer carries a "white card" with them, so they always have a pure white reference.

Entry level cameras may not have a white balance control and may automatically self-calibrate white balance through the dive. In this case, unusual color casts may need to be corrected in post-processing.

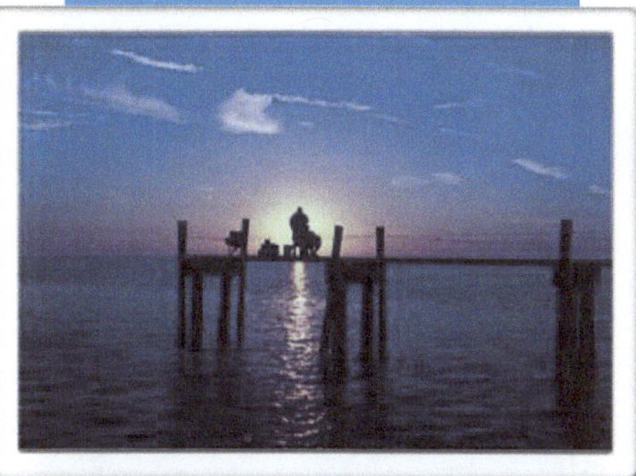

This photo shows the white balance adjusted to the cooler end of the spectrum.

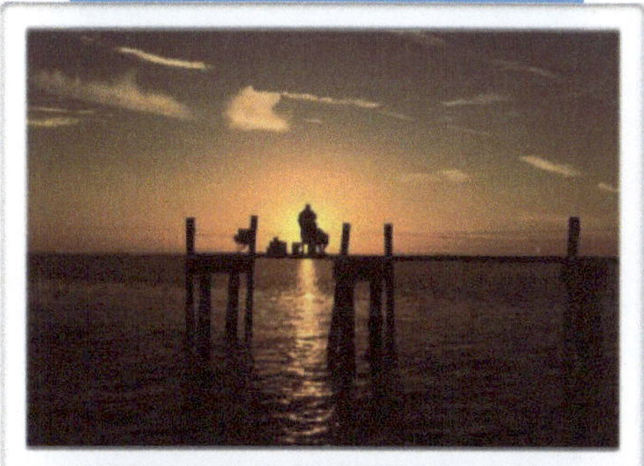

This photo shows a warm white balance with a lower color temperature.

In most cases the subtle choices of white balance are subjective choices which distinguish an artist's "look."

## White Balance

If you shoot RAW files, you can adjust white balance in post processing, however, if you begin with a proper white balance, like the top photo, your latitude for adjustment is far greater.
The lower two shots need significant post-processing to correct the various color casts.

### Using a White Card

A white balance card can be clipped to a diver's equipment, but care should be taken to ensure that it does not drag and damage the fragile environment. To use a white balance card, place it in front of your lens so that white fills the field of view. If you are mixing a combination of different diving lights, ensure a little of each of those lights is spilling onto the card. You do not need to focus on the card, since you are only telling the camera to register the color white in the current water conditions.

Do not cast a shadow on the card, and if you are in open water or in a cavern, make sure that ambient light is spilling onto the card. You should not see any hot spots, glare or shadows on the card, but rather a soft mix of light. You might have to tilt the card to catch a little ambient light or zoom in close to fill the field of view.

Once the light looks even, depress the white balance button on your camera housing. Most cameras will take a few seconds to sample the light. While it is sampling you may see a flashing icon. Once the icon stops flashing, you will be able to see the new color shift through the viewfinder. If your white card has a color bar on it, you can reference that to see if it looks accurate. If things do not appear as desired, then try to white balance again.

If you are diving in bright and shallow conditions in open water, you might need to use the grey side of the card to get an accurate white balance. Experiment with both sides of the card to see which gives you the best results.

If you use a card that is not white, it will vary the color cast of a photo. A light blue reference card will offer a warmer white balance that has a tinge of red. Professionals often use a light blue or 50% grey card to warm up flesh tones that tend to overexpose underwater.

If you are shooting RAW files, you may be able skip white balancing your camera, because the raw black and white sensor data is not applied permanently to the image until you post-process it in a computer and save it as a TIFF or JPEG file. When you first open a RAW file in its conversion program, you have the opportunity to try out different white balances and tints before committing them to the image.

However, if you get in the habit of white balancing your camera, then you will not risk saving a bad color cast because of a poorly calibrated screen or just because you did not notice. You'll also need less post processing and less time at the computer screen if you just shoot properly to begin with.

If you fail to white balance properly and are shooting in JPEG or TIFF formats, the improper white balance will be permanently applied to the original file. It is very difficult to restore the correct look in this case without loss of quality.

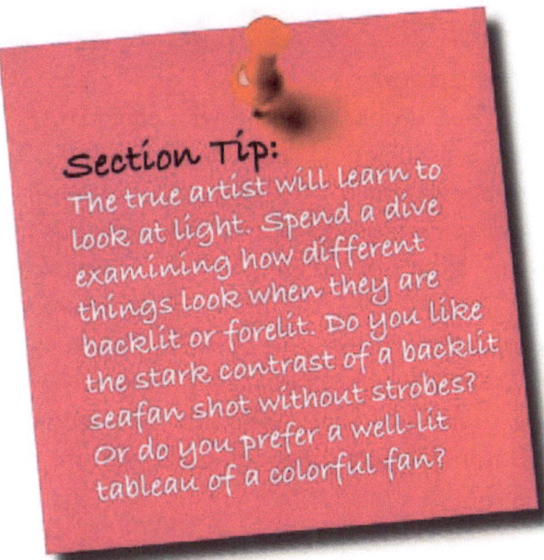


## Underwater Lighting

### Metering for Light

Many cameras are equipped with an internal light meter. When the shutter is depressed half-way, the photographer can see a bar graph that shows whether the shot is properly exposed. Review your specific camera instruction manual to learn how to properly use the light meter feature. Hand held light meters are preferred by some professionals who use the device to meter the light at the area of interest (like a model's face). By metering in this manner, the area of interest is correctly exposed. Some internal meters make their exposure choice based of several different samples and others operate be metering only the area just below center of the frame. Top level cameras give the photographer a choice between several different types of metering such as: center-weighted, matrix or spot metering.

### Balanced Exposures

The balanced exposure varies from a silhouette shot. One uses a strobe and the latter may not.

For a balanced underwater photo looking out of the doorway of an underwater cavern or wreck, meter the exposure to select a shutter speed that is long enough to expose the background of the beautiful light filtering through the cavern or wreck. But the foreground must also be burned into the image by flashing a strobe, which seers in the details of the foreground or model. The strobe will only fire for a spilt second, since its light is very powerful. The key thing to remember, is while the strobe illuminates the foreground details, the shutter speed and aperture will determine the background illumination.

If you are using a model, then the proper exposure will fill the background with a beautiful blue water backdrop and the strobe will illuminate the model and cast light into their dive mask.

### Backscatter

All underwater environments have varying degrees of turbidity. Small particles floating in the water column obscure visibility to some degree or another. When we light up these particles with a strobe that hits them head-on, then they look like large white dots in the resulting photograph.

To avoid backscatter, you can either shoot without a flash or put a strobe on a moveable arm. When using an arm system, the photographer can manipulate the angle at which light strikes the subject. Choosing a 45-degree angle will usually eliminate backscatter issues.

## Sync Speed

When strobes are used with cameras, there is usually a minimum shutter speed that allows time for the camera to meter and send a firing command to the strobe. Many older traditional SLRs have a sync speed of 1/125 or 1/250 second. Newer models have faster sync speeds of up to 1/500th second. If the photographer selects a faster shutter speed, then the strobe will not fire quickly enough to register in the shot.

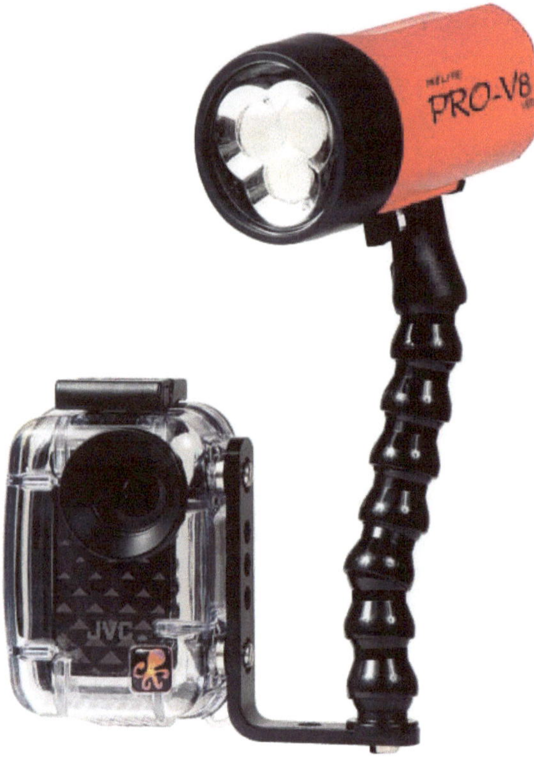


Many older model strobes are not capable of synchronizing with new digital cameras, so be careful about combining cameras and strobes from different vintages. Still other strobes are equipped with a selector switch that will recognize a pre-fire over a full-fire and will synchronize at the correct moment. Check your instruction manual for compatibility with different cameras.

## Using a Single Strobe

When you begin using a single strobe, start slow to learn about the capabilities of your equipment. The best way to understand the parameters of the power of your strobe is to just go shoot in the open water.

Once you venture into the overhead environment like a cavern, shooting in an automatic mode will rarely result in a balanced exposure and strobes set to TTL will not yield the best results. Most stunning cave or wreck photos have utilized multiple slave strobes with carefully chosen manual exposures.

Set your strobe arm so that the light hits the subject on an angle and use a primary dive light with a soft video reflector to provide light for focusing and to illuminate difficult areas like the eyes in the diver's mask. If you are dexterous, you can hand-hold your primary light. If not, you might want to secure it the housing or arm system to free your workload. If you fix the modeling light to the housing or arm system, try to place it opposite the strobe so it will fill in harsh shadows. Beware that you do not create backscatter from placing it at a frontal angle.

As you adjust the position of the strobe arm, you will find that each foot of distance from the subject equates roughly to an f-stop change in exposure. If you are getting too much power from a strobe, you can either manually select a lower power output, or simply move it a foot further from the subject.

## Dual Strobe Photography

The ideal, basic set-up includes strobes mounted on either side of a camera housing. These strobes can be operated with a dual sync cord or with a single sync and manual controller/slave sensor unit.

Each strobe is extended as far away from the housing body as possible and angled towards the subject. Both strobes

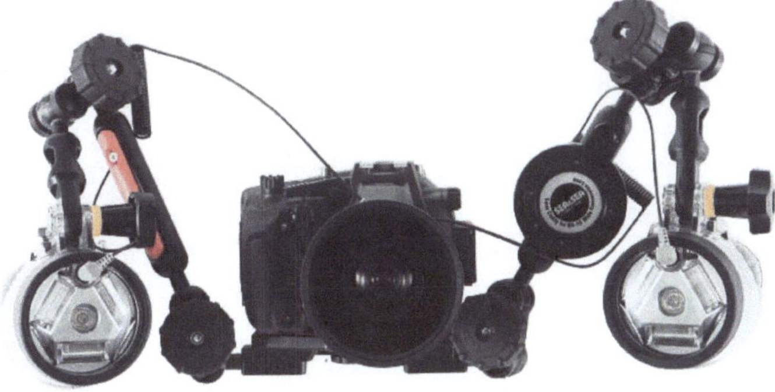

may be used to full capacity in a dark scenario or one may be used at full power with the second softening harsh shadows. Some people use a lower-powered secondary strobe, if it is only needed to remove harsh shadows.

**Slave Strobes**

Slave strobes are independent strobes that are either hand-held, placed in a location or mounted on camera arms. Slave strobes are not physically linked to the camera with an electrical sync cord. Slave strobes are triggered by a flash of light. When the primary strobe fires, it trips the slave strobe to fire quickly enough to be registered in the shot.

If you are in a dark environment, like a cave or a wreck, your primary dive light can cause unwanted firing of your slave strobe, so the utmost care must be taken with quick light movements. For this reason, it is wise to swim to a photo location with the slave turned off, then power it up when you are ready to set up the shot. Bright sunlight can also trigger a slave strobe, so it is advisable to power them down before surfacing at the end of a dive.

Most slaves can be dialed up or down for sensitivity, but I have found that I require the highest degree of sensitivity in most cases.

Some strobes have slave sensors that are built into the face of the strobe. Although this can be a useful feature, the creative photographer will need slave sensors that are independent from the strobe head. When slaves are hand-held by the model, you will want to be able to point the sensor towards the camera and the strobe in a different direction. This maximizes sensing distance and allows the diver to hide the strobe itself. Some of the newest slave strobes, such as Inon strobes, feature a 360° sensor that claims to be able to sense a flash in any direction.

## Dazzling Beauty

In 1996, I was a part of a large team of explorers who were unlocking the secrets of Sistema Dos Ojos in Mexico's Yucatan peninsula. We camped in the jungle at a spot called M1 and spooled out reams of line in some of the most decorated caves I had ever seen. It was always a dilemma to decide whether to drop a thousand feet of line or go take photos. We only had enough power to charge a few lights each night, so the photo shoot was a one-shot deal. If we wanted to shoot again, it would require a seven km hike out of the jungle to the Hidden Worlds Dive Shop for proper charging.

Paul Heinerth and I decided to shoot the cathedral-like room called Pierre's Palace. We swam our cameras with seven Ikelite slave strobes back into the labyrinth. The delicate strobes in those days were not as reliable as they are today. Getting more than half of them to work properly at one time was a victory. When we arrived at the location, we gingerly swam and placed the slaves throughout the room, hiding the units, but revealing the slave eye. While placing the last 300 watt strobe, an errant flash of a primary light triggered a slave and launched an endless cascade of firing pulses around us. My retinas were burning as the terminal firing loop continued. We quickly swam around to turn off the offending units, silting the entire tableau and ruining our chances for a shot. By the time the strobes were turned off, there was not enough battery power remaining for any decent shots. Two cameras, seven strobes, a day of hiking and a swim through the cave and not much to show for the effort. Priceless.

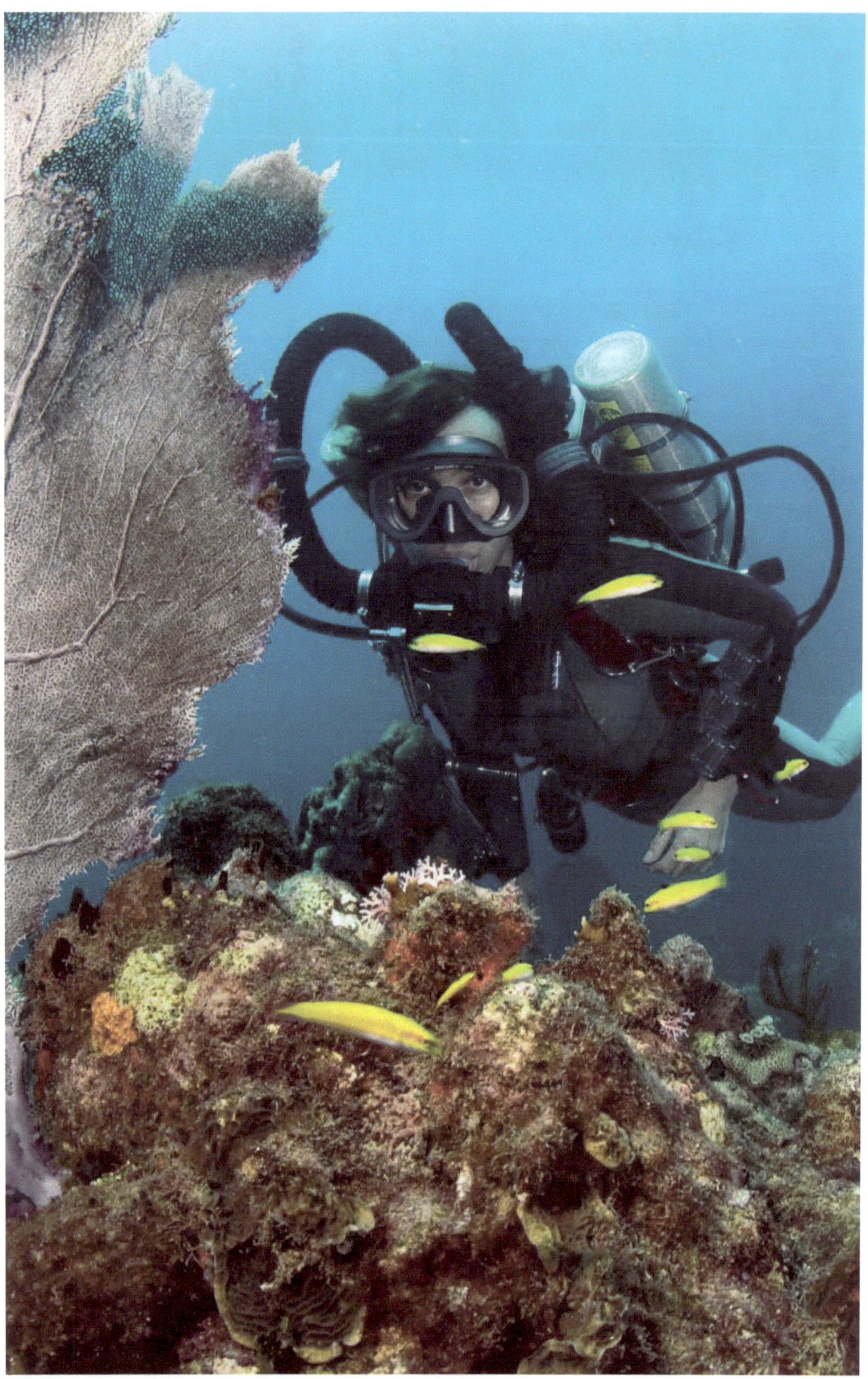

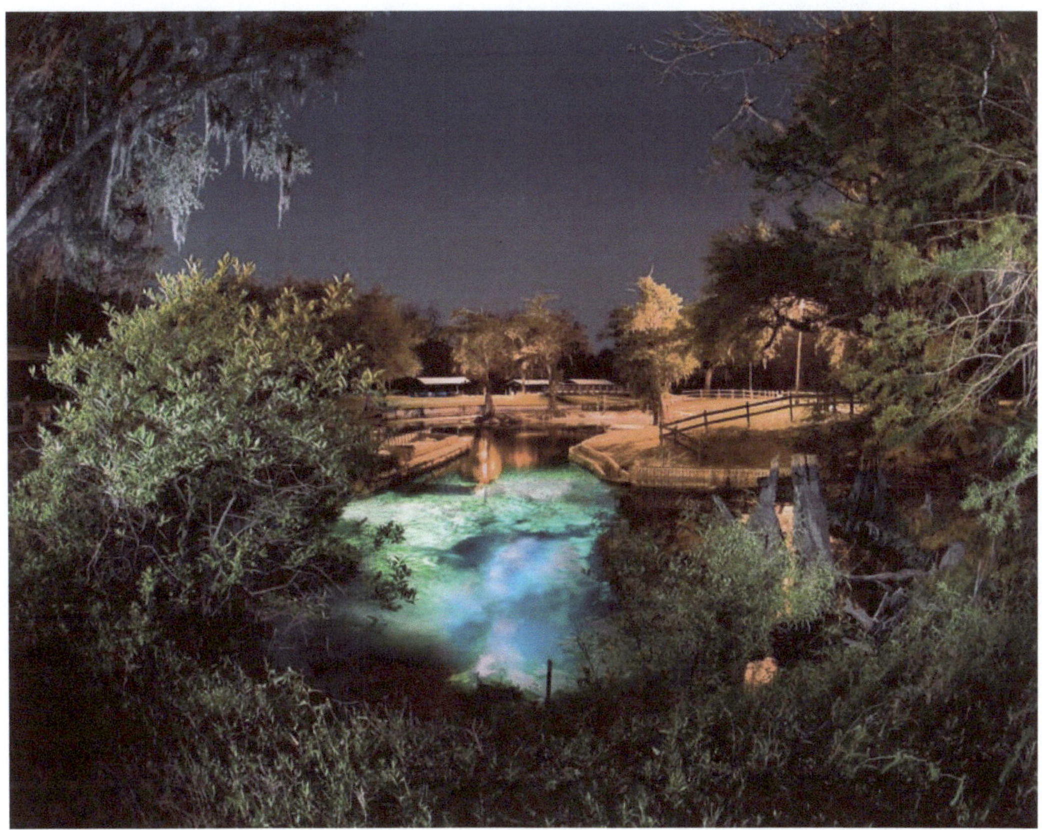

Giving your frame a distinct foreground, middle and back gives a shot dimension and helps to frame the model's reference.

Topside shots enhance your portfolio and give you opportunity to practice creative techniques. This long exposure is illuminated with a diver firing strobes in the water. The exposure is so lengthy that the diver does not register in the scene. After practicing this on land, there is no reason that you could not apply the same technique on a wreck or a reef dive.

workflow

## Section Seven



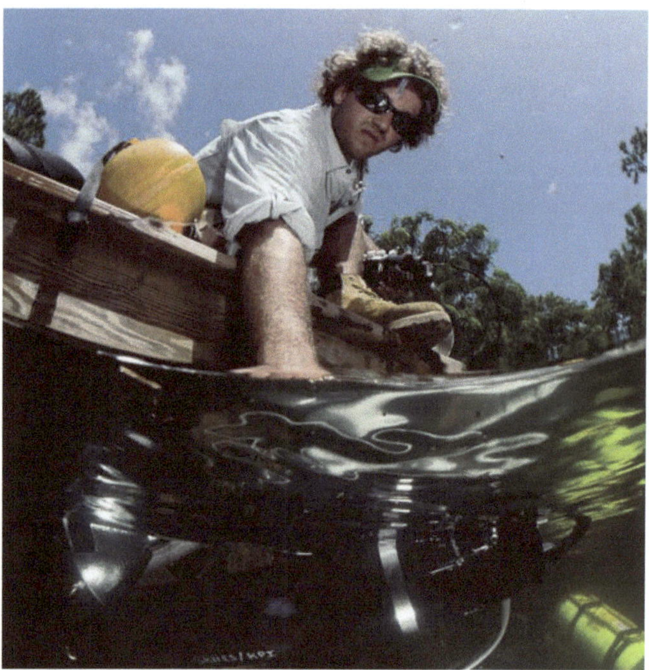

# Digital Workflow Steps

Digital workflow is a term used to describe the preparation and processing steps that are included in your day of photography.

### Set-Up

The first step in digital workflow is to properly set the parameters of your camera. Prior to placing the camera in its housing you should make decisions about file format, resolution, exposure and focusing. Your memory card should be emptied or re-formatted and you should test fire the camera.

Before your first outing, go to the camera menu that allows you to set your image counter. Add your initials and set the counter to "0." Tell the camera menu that you want all photos to be named in succession and not reset every time you replace the memory card in the camera. Each of your images will now have a unique sequential number like, "JEH_0002345.RAW."

### Confirmation

The second step is to place the camera in the housing and check all necessary controls. After the strobes are connected and powered-up, a test shot should confirm proper function of the camera and synchronization with the strobes.

**Downloading**

The third step in the digital workflow process happens after the dive and involves downloading the images from the camera for storage on a computer or one or more hard disks or DVDs.

There are two ways to download images from your camera to your computer. Each technique has its inherent advantages and disadvantages.

**• USB Connection**

Connecting the camera to the computer via USB port is preferred by some since there is little risk of damaging the memory card since it is never taken out of the camera. The card slot is also kept very clean since it is rarely opened. The disadvantage is that a voltage spike through your computer may damage the computer, the camera and the images on the card. When traveling in locations with unreliable power, it is worth keeping this in mind. Similarly, a sudden loss of camera battery power could result in lost or corrupted data.

**• Using Card Readers**

Once you have removed the memory card from your camera, it can be inserted into a card reader that hooks up to the USB port on your computer. In this case a power spike could damage the computer and card reader, but not the camera. The drawback of card readers is that their inexpensive technology sometimes fails and this could result in loss of data and photos. However, if you shoot a lot of photos, you can download photos from multiple readers simultaneously. The newest cameras offer wireless transfer of images to your computer or the Internet.

Many cameras come with proprietary software that launches automatically as soon as you plug in the USB port. It is not necessary to use these programs. Your memory card is just like a hard drive. It will

## Techno History

In the mid 1980s, I worked for the student services office at my university. We had a small Mac 128K on which to create posters and forms. The venerable Fine Arts Faculty were deeply conflicted over new technology versus traditional methods. I even learned to set lead type at an old Carriage House in downtown Toronto. Puttering away on that new Mac, I dreamed of where the experimental program of "Hypertext" would take us.

It wasn't until 1990, that the editing software program Photoshop would hit the streets. By this time, I was founder and Art Director of a fresh, dynamic graphic design studio. We bought our first Mac laptops and the blindingly-fast, Quadra computers in 1991 and vowed to keep ahead of the technology curve. Type was output on our massive Linotype machines. We would complete an ad layout, send the full color art to the beast in the corner and then, keeping our fingers crossed, we hoped to find four-color separated film in the basket the following morning. Even with the fastest processor chips of our time, output would take a painful 24-48 hours to emerge from the magic box.

I was teaching others how to leverage the new technology and manipulate their photography, but we were still shooting on film, scanning the images, and outputting on film for the press. We were saving money and time, but suffering several levels of image degradation along the way.

After experiences like these, there can be no question about why I am so excited about the technology that we have at our finger tips today. With a digital camera and laptop, you can run a modern ad agency that dwarfs the client capability I had in those early days of my career. Companies like Nike Canada, Labatt's Brewery, Canon Camera and IBM flocked to our doors, but today, I can offer more digital services, sitting in my pajamas, with my feet up by the fireplace and no staff at all.

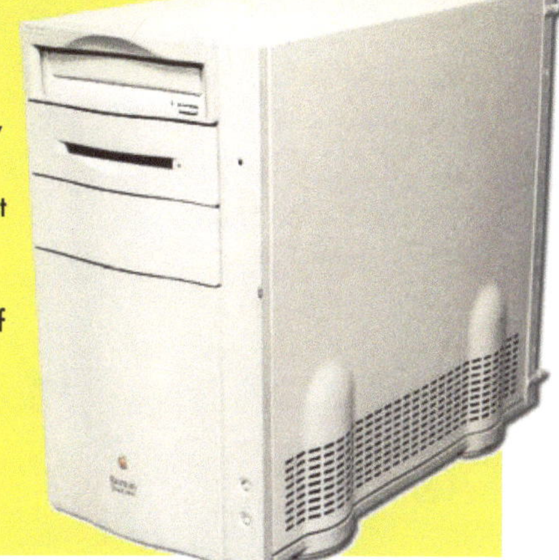

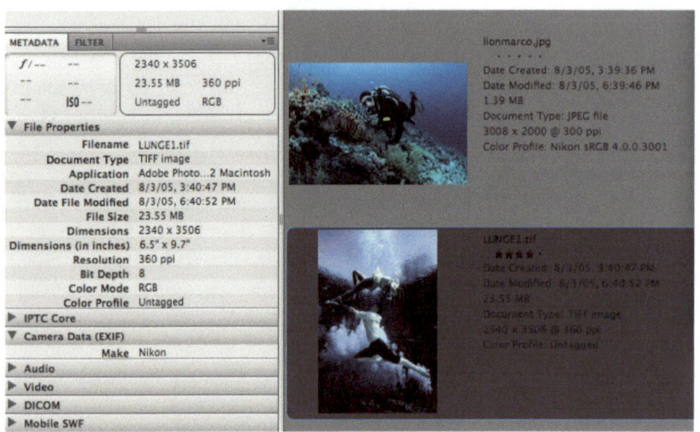


Take time to properly organize your files and add your personal copyright data and other metadata tags that will help you keep track of shots in the future.

appear on your desktop and you can simply drag the files from the card to either your computer or an external hard drive.

You can simultaneously drag and drop the photos to a computer and an external hard drive so that you have an immediate back-up of your files. Many people also make DVD back-ups, but if you do so, you should recopy those DVDs every couple of years or so. Do not consider DVDs to be permanent, archival storage.

Once the images are downloaded from the memory card, it is preferable to reformat the card rather than simply deleting the files. When you delete a file, there are remnants left on a card since you have only truly deleted the index and not all the data. The remaining artifacts also take up critical space on the card. It is advisable to reformat to maximize available space and lessen the chance of file corruption down the road.

## Organizing and Sorting Your Files

The fourth step in the digital workflow process involves organizing your files with metadata. Many programs like Adobe Lightroom or Bridge allow you to add keywords to the image file by either typing in words or checking boxes of commonly used keywords like "cave" or "shark." You can get as detailed as you wish with keywords, but critical information like location, model's name, etc. should always be noted so that you may search for an image with those keywords later.

Programs like Bridge will also allow you to append copyright templates, project names, and other data and will automatically list exposure, date, time, lens type, whether the flash fired, etc.

## Editing the Image

One of the biggest advantages of shooting digitally, is the opportunity to immediately edit the original photo. Step five in the digital workflow is editing. If you shoot in RAW format, the file itself already carries an adjustable range of data that is much like shooting bracketed shots on film. Each RAW image contains several stops of

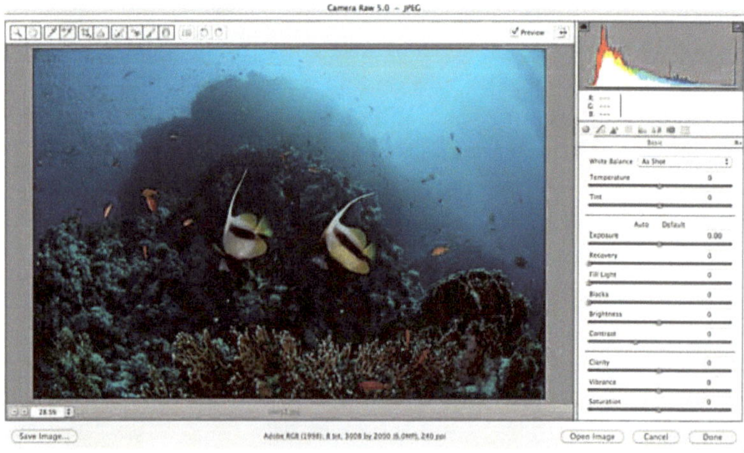

information. We can open a RAW file and adjust down for the bright areas of the photo. You can open a RAW file and pull up the shadows. You can open it and pick an exposure in the mid-range of levels. Each pixel has been recorded with a vast range of brightness that can be raised and lowered as long as you have not clipped either end of the histogram.

Most professional photographers will agree that Photoshop Creative Suite is the industry's best image editing software. Coupled with Adobe Bridge or Lightroom, it can make a powerful and fast workflow possible.

Using Adobe Bridge or Lightroom as a browser you can open a single file or groups of files. The files are opened quickly in a RAW conversion. The editor can apply simple changes to a single file or to a batch of files simultaneously. If the entire group of photos needs to have the color temperature changed, this can be done simultaneously. Powerful "auto" defaults are available for color balance and exposure or each individual file can be tweaked. Once a group of images is manipulated, then they can be either saved with changes or opened in Photoshop for full image editing capability. Changes made to RAW files are viewable in Lightroom and are non-destructive to the original file data.

### Saving the Image

After the image has been edited and retouched, it is important to give the image a new unique name while preserving the original numerical data. As an example, I suggest naming files in the following way:

"MarySmithHartSpringJEH0002345.TIF" or "whalecalfDRJEH0002987.jpg" with DR being my short form for Dominican Republic and JEH, my initials.

## The Wailing Wall

My formal photography education began in a studio at York University in 1983. I had been shooting casually my whole life and owned an enviable Pentax camera system that was purchased from my father. The competition for this fine arts program was brutal, and I was a little intimidated by my flamboyant classmates in those days. My first year class of 150 eager, young, artistic souls yielded only a dozen, fourth-year graduates of the Visual Communications Design Program. I reasoned that my classmates with spiked technicolor mohawks would never get the graduate's cap over their thorny coifs. But, in the end, it was my odd and tormented professor that intimidated me the most.

I slapped a wet print on the "wailing wall" and waited for my mentor to tell me it was worthless. He was brilliant, but often intoxicated, and his critiques were often traumatic. I had just finished yet another package of 8x10 photo paper and wondered how I could afford the next one. Another bartending shift? Sell my treasured Papasan chair? I had printed that negative over 100 times, carefully burning and dodging the highlights and shadows while streaming endlessly through the shadowy doors of the darkroom. Enlarger, developer, stop bath, fixer, wash, hang, coffee, wailing wall, bathroom. Repeat.

Seasonal affective disorder in the long winter days of my Canadian homeland was bad enough, but when the few hours of daylight are spent in a photo lab, your skin morphs to a Vitamin D-deprived shade similar to fish. But this time, as I awaited the torture brought on by his third coffee mug of professorial Glenfiddich, he said, "brilliant." Flattered and invigorated, I gratefully accepted his encouragement, but turned down his request to model nude in his private studio. His demeanor was contemptible enough, but modeling didn't seem to raise the grades of my girl friends in class. That photo eventually led to a small feature in Photographer's Who's Who and a new confidence to continue my creative pursuits.

What this experience taught me, was that persistence is the secret route to professional stature. The only way to learn, is to shoot a lot and accept criticism. Quality will come through quantity, as long as you carefully continue to examine, critique and expand your knowledge.

By adding this sort of information in the name of the file, it makes the file easier to search and find later.

Now you will have an original RAW file that can be retouched in a different way later and a matching master file that has been edited and retouched and saved as a TIFF or JPG file. Since you will not have the time or desire to edit and retouch every file you shoot, only your "selects" will have a unique file name.

Always retain the numerical data in your file names, so that you can find the matching RAW file if needed at a later date.

If you use Lightroom, this data is saved as an edit to the original RAW file, and the original default is stored and may be reviewed at any time.

## Sharing, Printing and Distributing Images

The final step in digital workflow is to share, print and/or distribute your images through web sites, high resolution prints, slide shows, online galleries, image banks, email, etc.

### • Internet Storage and Sharing

Since computer screens can only display 72 dpi, there is no need to use high resolution images for display on web sites. More importantly, if you send high resolution images via the Internet, they will take a long time to load on a web page or transmit via email. High resolution images may also be pirated and used by third parties without your knowledge.

When you want to send a photo by email or post it on a web page, decide on dimensions suitable for a computer screen, then save that size at 72 dpi. Many programs offer "batch automation of files" where you can tell a program to take every image in a folder and save it as a JPEG file or a given dimension. With these programs you can simply walk away while an entire folder is processed in your absence.

The new smaller files should retain the same name as their parent file, but a unique letter should be added at the end so the file is not mistaken for the full resolution file. Every small file can be named in the following way:

"MarySmithHartSprgJEH002345s.JPG" or "whalecalfDRJEH0002987s.JPG," with "s" indicating small.

Files for email should be saved as JPG for quick transmission. Websites are compatible with either JPEG or GIF formats.

Many programs like Photoshop will also allow the photographer to add a "watermark" to their image. Watermarks are subtle words or images placed on the photograph that obscure part of the picture. They protect the photographer from piracy, but some people do not understand that if they purchase your photo, you will be sending them something without the garish watermark!

### • Printing Fulfillment

Home printers are available in every price and quality range, but outside services are also available for digital photographers. Any traditional photo processor is capable of printing your digital files. JPG files are universally acceptable, but many studios can also handle other formats.

Fulfillment websites like SmugMug, Flicker and others, are also popping up everywhere. You can store a folder of images on a fulfillment site and then allow either public access or password access to a particular folder. People that have the password can view the photo album, make selections and order copies of the photos. You can assign a royalty to the price of the photo, and the web site provider will send you a check when your balance reaches a certain level.

Soccer Moms all over the country are starting simple businesses by sharing their photos online and allowing other parents to download and purchase prints through fulfillment sites. Dive resort photographers are doing the same thing for additional revenue and guest satisfaction.

Specialty sites, like CafePress will also allow viewers to purchase products like coffee mugs, posters, t-shirts and ornaments with photographs from online albums. In this case, the photographer sets up the album and chooses the royalty percentage to be added to the product purchase. The web site takes care of fulfilling the order and shipping to the customer, so that the photographer never needs to stock inventory.

## Gurus and Mentors

Nikonos underwater cameras have been around since the 1960s. It wasn't until 1990, that I bought my own shiny new Nikonos V. I was traveling to a tropical destination and reasoned that I might be able to purchase a unit there at a better price than I could find in Toronto. The Canadian dollar wasn't too healthy at the time, so I loaded $4500 into my pants pocket with the intention of buying an entire package of gear. That was well over twice the value of my trusty Toyota Tercel at the time.

I walked into a well-known, underwater photo school and began looking around. The money was burning a hole in my pocket and I couldn't wait to trade it for the bright orange camera. I began making a mental list of things that I coveted in this place. Finally, the guru emerged from the office and asked if I needed some assistance. I nodded an affirmative and said that I had several questions. After a brief pause, I was handed a small business card that read, "You have one free question. Beyond that, you'll need to sign up for my class." I was horrified. I had intended on not only buying a camera system, but also a class. Instead, I asked one question, dropped my mental list in the doorway and retreated as quickly as possible.

I bought my Nikonos V camera on a snowy, winter's day in Toronto after I got home and used it to shoot ice diving instead of tropical fish. A year later, I sought out a photo assistant from the same photo school and hired her for private lessons. Through her, I learned that even a formal university arts education doesn't help much underwater. The training with her was money well spent.

Whenever eager young people approach me with enthusiastic questions about technical diving or photography, I always remember how I felt that day long ago, when my potential mentor snubbed me.

Ask as many questions as you like, my answers may not be what you bargained for, but they are always free.

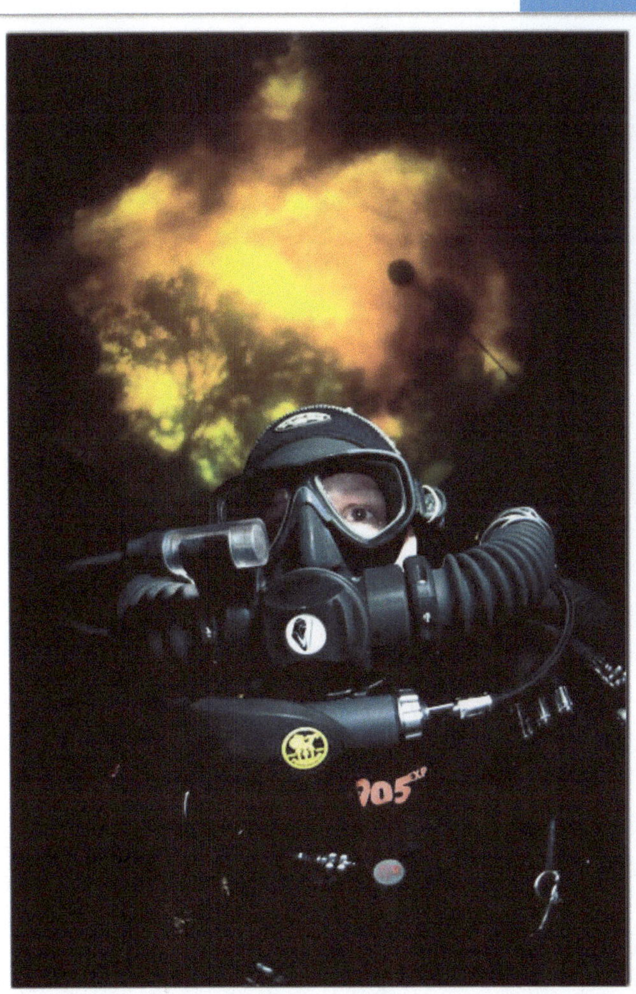

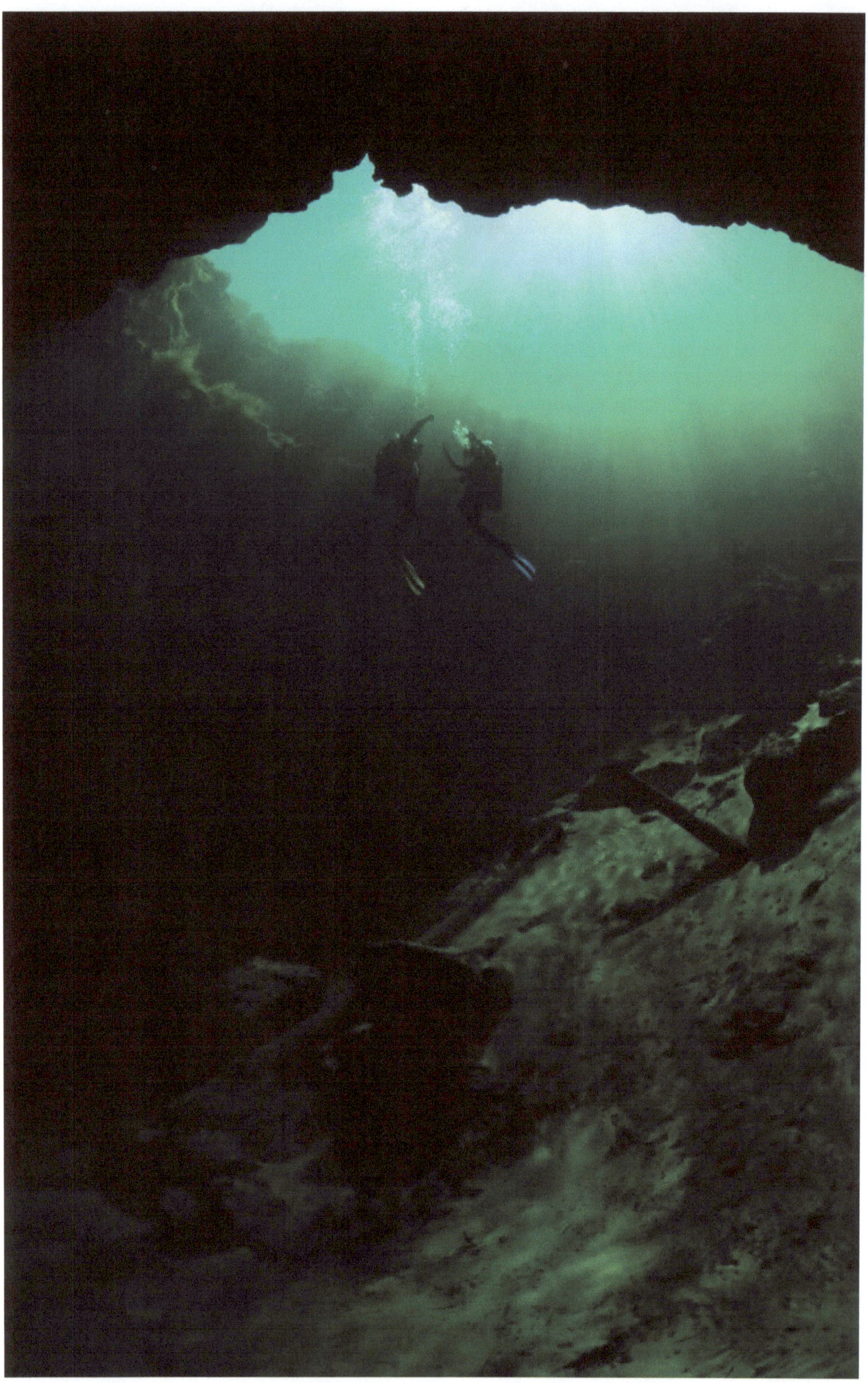

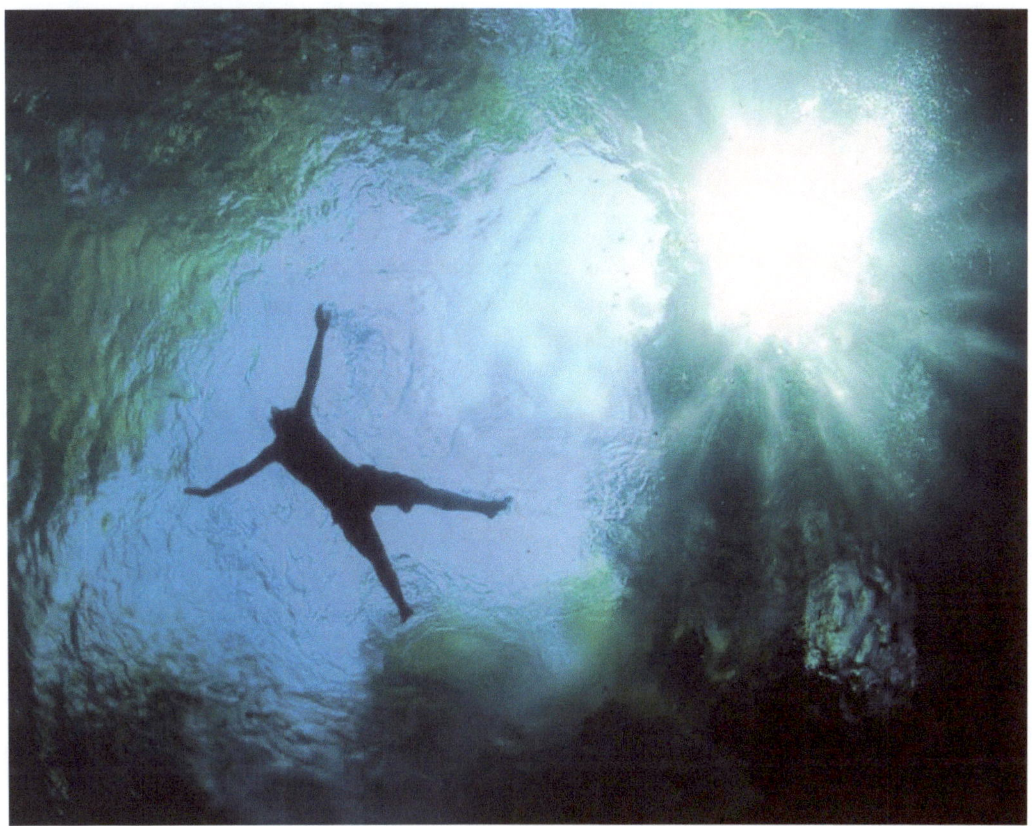

The photo on the facing page shows effective capture of the beams of sunlight. The small divers in the scene give a great, vastness to the shot. Remember to shoot vertically for variety and to enhance the sensation of depth.

The swimmer silhouetted against the flare of sun shows how breaking the rules of exposure can still be artistic. Even thought the sun has flared and clipped the white highlights, the overall effect is of a tranquil watercolor painting.

appendix

Contents



## Diving Skills Development

### Suggested Sequence

Follow the suggested sequence of skills, moving on as mastery is achieved. Some skills will not apply to all camera systems. The following list is not intended to be completed in one dive, but should take several excursions and repeated practice. Consider these as general photo assignments to give you goals to practice in any underwater environment.

### Review Camera Settings

Before getting anywhere near the water, ensure that you are familiar with your camera settings and the various knobs and dials on your housing, which may or may not be labelled on the exterior.

### Assembly

Take your time to carefully clean and assemble your system without the time pressure of preparing for a dive.

### Test Fire

Test fire the camera to ensure that strobes fire properly. Check that the camera will focus and ensure you haven't left the lens cap on the camera in a housing! Check the function of all critical knobs and buttons to ensure that everything is aligned properly in the camera housing.

### Leak Check

After assembling and testing your system as per manufacturer's instructions, slowly submerge your camera in fresh water, watching for bubbles that may indicate a leak. You may need to turn on the camera to activate a leak alarm as necessary.

### Trim and Weight Modifications

After successful completion of a leak check, swim with your camera system to experience the drag and task load of carrying a large object. Hover motionless and use breath control to try to rise and lower yourself into position without silting or damaging the environment. Determine whether you will need to add either buoyant camera arms or lead weight to the system in order to achieve comfort and neutral buoyancy.

## White Balance

If your camera is capable of white balancing, do so using a white card and take a few test shots. White balance again using a neutral grey or light blue card and take test shots.

## Looking at Ambient Light

If your camera system is equipped with a flash unit or external strobes, turn them to the off position. Using automatic or preprogrammed camera settings, hover neutrally in the water column and take a series of photographs beginning by looking up and rotating so that you can observe the difference between sunlight over your shoulder, looking directly into the sun and side-lighting an object or model. Take a series of shots looking horizontally at the same object or model. Finally, take a series of shots looking down on the same object or model. When you examine the series of shots, you should review the difference between shooting at different angles and the effects of different light directions. Analyze how various angles of sunlight either accentuate or reduce backscatter. Look carefully at how light falling on the front of an object looks different than side light, which accentuates edges and adds dimension to a subject. If you are using a model, this series of shots will help you to improve buoyancy skills and communication techniques.

## Using a Single Strobe

If your camera is equipped with a flash unit or single strobe, turn it on for this dive. If the strobe is mounted on an arm, try to angle the strobe to cast a beam at an angle towards your subject. Using automatic settings on your camera and TTL settings on your strobe, experiment with shooting at different angles to your subject. If you are shooting in open water, rotate around to utilize different sun angles for different results.

## Using Dual Strobes

If your camera is equipped with dual strobes, position them on either side of the housing at an angle to the subject. Think of one strobe as the primary light source and the other as a fill flash, that removes shadows from the subject. Take a series of shots using an automatic exposure before moving on to aperture or shutter priority described below. Begin your shooting with the TTL mode on strobes and then slowly begin experimenting with different power settings if your strobe is capable of changing output. After each shot, review the LCD screen for composition and the histogram for exposure. Adjust accordingly after each shot.

## Aperture Priority

If your camera is capable of shooting in Aperture Priority mode, select an aperture of f/8 and let the camera select the shutter speed. If your histogram indicates underexposure, then shift to a larger aperture, such as f/5.6 or larger. Experiment by changing exposure compensation in either a positive or negative direction to fine tune the histogram.

## Shutter Priority

If your camera is capable of shooting in Shutter Priority mode, select a shutter speed of 1/60th second and let the camera select the aperture. If your histogram indicates underexposure, then see if you can hold the camera still at 1/30th second. Experiment by changing exposure compensation in either a positive or negative direction to fine tune the histogram.

## Manual Photography

If your camera allows for full manual control, experiment with different f-stops and shutter speeds. Although it may seem a waste to ignore pre-set options, this method of photography allows for the greatest creative freedom.

## Macro Photography

Macro photography is a type of shooting that brings the viewer in close to magnify small items to a full frame of view. The following settings will give you a starting point for beginning your adventures with macro photography.

### Compact Cameras

1. If your camera has a macro mode, turn the selector switch to this mode.
2. If your camera comes with framing arms, known as "goal posts," install them to assist in framing the shot and getting the correct depth of field.
3. Turn on the flash or strobe unit.
4. Focus using spot focus mode and select a part of the frame like the head or eye of a creature.
5. Use the lowest ISO available, such as 100, to enhance color saturation and sharpness.
6. If your camera has a Manual Exposure Mode, begin using f/8 and 1/1000th second shutter speed.
7. If your camera has Aperture Priority Mode, you may select f/8 and allow the camera to select the shutter speed appropriate for the shot.
8. Experiment with different strobe angles if your strobe is external.
9. Bracket your shots.

### DSLR Cameras

1. Turn on the strobe unit. If you have dual strobes, turn on both, but lower the power output on one side.
2. Focus using spot focus mode and select a part of the frame like the head or eye of the subject.
3. Use the lowest ISO available, such as 100, to enhance color saturation and sharpness.
4. Use a small aperture like f/22 to maximize depth of field. If you are using a 105 mm lens, select an even smaller aperture.
5. Experiment with different manual strobe powers and f-stops. You will learn to vary these as you shoot different subjects and different distances.

## Troubleshooting

- **"No card" warning:**

You forgot to put the memory card in the slot before diving. Test fire your camera before entering the water to avoid this common mistake. Consider downloading your shots with a USB cable instead of a card reader.

- **Too much backscatter:**

**Solution for compact cameras -**

If your camera has an internal flash that is used to trigger a fiber-optic external flash, try putting a piece of duct tape on the outside of the housing, thus blocking the internal flash from appearing in the shot, while still allowing it to trigger the second unit. This will reduce backscatter by removing the front flash.

**Solution for all external strobes -**

Increase the angle of the light hitting the subject and reduce anything that illuminates your shot head-on.

- **All my shots are underexposed:**

Learn how to review histograms underwater. Use the LCD screen to evaluate composition only and use the histogram to evaluate your exposure.

- **Flat colors:**

**Solution for compact cameras -**

You really need to get close to your subject and likely within 2-3 feet or closer. If you are not getting the field of view that you wish to achieve, then try adding an externally mounted wide angle lens that will increase the field of vision and allow you to get closer to the subject, thus lessening the filtration effects of the water column.

**Solution for all cameras -**

Everyone benefits by getting closer to the subject with wide angle lenses or adding more strobe power to your system. Distance reduces color, sharpness and contrast.

- **Photos are pixellated:**

Use the finest setting that your camera allows and shoot in RAW mode if possible.

- **Shots are not focussed properly:**

Use the movable spot focus to snap the focus on a particular area of your shot like the diver's eyes or the face of a macro critter rather than always focusing in the center of the screen. Review focus underwater in your viewfinder by enlarging the preview to 100% magnification, if your camera allows.

- **Motion blur:**

It is tough to hold the camera still enough to shoot any slower than 1/60th second. If your subject is stationary you may get away with 1/30th second. Exhale first and take the shot at the end of the exhale cycle and be prepared for shutter lag on inexpensive cameras.

- **Photo looks red:**

Your white balance is likely set incorrectly or you may be trying to use a red filter with a flash. Red filters may only be used without flashes and strobes.

- **Flat composition:**

Try to create a shot with a beautiful foreground and a background. The layers give the shot the illusion of three dimensions.

- **Lack of variety:**

Few people remember to shoot vertically at all, and this is the format that gives the greatest illusion of depth.

- **Fish butts:**

Don't chase animals around the reef. Remain still and allow the reef to accept your presence as unthreatening.

- **Composition looks "busy":**

Get low and shoot at an upward angle. This will fill the background with a graduated blue field that simplifies the composition and gives your shot the illusion of depth.

- **Model does not seem engaged in the shot:**

Try to accentuate the diver's eyes in the photo by focusing on the eyes and illuminating them with either the flash/strobe or an additional hand-held light.

Instruct the diver to look at something like a fish, rather than directly into the lens of the camera.

- **Specks or "noise" in the shot:**

Use a lower ISO number if possible or increase the light/flash in the shot. Open the aperture further if available.

- **Camera or lens is fogging:**

Never put a cool, air-conditioned camera into a hot, humid housing. Either load in your hotel room or acclimatize the housing, camera and lenses to the environment before loading. Carefully use fresh, desiccant packs in small compact housings. Never leave your housing in direct sunlight. Keep it cool and cover it with a wet towel on the boat.

- **Ghostly gears in shot:**

Depending on the angle that you are shooting, sun can reflect on a dome port and show up in your shot as a ghostly circular bracket. Some scratches are also accentuated when the sun hits them at a particular angle. Reshoot using a different angle.

- **Poor visibility:**
  Shoot silhouette images, black and white shots or switch to macro photography for the day. Close shooting with a wide angle lens will also make the water appear clearer than you might imagine.

- **Camera flooded:**
  Prevention is the key. Common causes are improper assembly, O-ring damage, pet hair and desiccant packs caught in the housing door. All O-ring grooves need careful maintenance with removal of salt crystals that may build up over time. Check all strobe fittings, battery doors, dome ports and doors for proper fit before the leak test. Ensure latches are fully closed. Carefully conduct a leak test before taking the plunge. Ask a Divemaster to pass the camera to you in the water rather than jumping in with your camera in hand.

- **Sync cord stuck:**
  Avoid this by removing and cleaning contacts often. Use a product like Salt-X to prevent salt crystals from seizing the fitting permanently. Use electronic contact cleaner on the fitting if corrosion is present.

- **Dome Port Scratch:**
  If your dome port is acrylic, the scratch may be polished out with a "Micro-Mesh" kit. Glass ports are impossible to polish, but many scratches will be invisible and will "fill" with water, only appearing at a few unique sun angles. Clean domes with lint-free lens paper or special lens cloths.

## Glossary of Terms

### Ambient light
Natural light photography illuminated only by the sun.

### Field of view
A measure of the width of your shot sometimes expressed in degrees.

### Aperture
Circular opening behind your lens which admits light like the iris of an eyeball. Diameter changes as you change your f-stop.

### Aperture priority
"A" on a camera mode dial, is a setting on some cameras that allows the user to choose a specific aperture value, while the camera selects a shutter speed to match.

### Artifacts
A visible error in a pixel or series of pixels. It is the result of an aggressive data compression scheme that discards some data in order to make file smaller.

### Backscatter
Unintended specks of light appearing when the light from a strobe or flash unit hits them head on, thus reflecting them back into the camera.

### Bracketing
Shooting a subject several times with different settings.

### Buffer
Temporary storage that holds an image or images before they are written to a memory card.

### Color temperature
A number, in degrees Kelvin, that represents the approximate color of the light or the appearance of white. Higher numbers are bluer and cooler, while lower numbers are warmer and more reddish yellow.

### Contrast
The range of difference between the lightest and darkest part of the shot.

**DOF or Depth of field**
It's the area of an image that appears sharp or in focus.

**Desiccant**
Chemical packet that absorbs moisture.

**DSLR**
Digital single lens reflex camera.

**EXIF**
Exchangeable Image File Format.

**Exposure compensation**
A feature used to adjust the automatically calculated exposure. Compensation can be either positive (additional exposure) or negative (reduced exposure).

**Fast lens**
Lens with an aperture of f/2.8 or larger, which performs well in low light conditions.

**f-stop**
The pupil diameter of the aperture of the camera.

**Fiber optic cable**
A thin cable placed in front of a flash unit on the outside of a housing, which is used to trigger an independent strobe.

**Fill light**
Subtle light which illuminates a subject without overpowering the background.

**Focal length**
The focal length of a lens determines the magnification at which it images distant objects.

**Focus light**
A light that assists the photographer with underwater focus. Advanced models may dim when the camera strobe fires.

**Full frame sensor**
A camera with a sensor that is equivalent size and ratio to 35mm film stock.

**Guide number**
A number that represents the relative power of a strobe.

**Hot shoe**
The accessory slot on top of a camera that accepts the electronic connection in a housing or an external flash on land.

**Iris**
See aperture.

**ISO**
Acronym for International Standards Organization. Used to indicate film speed or sensor sensitivity.

**JPEG**
Acronym for Joint Photographic Experts Group. The most common file format, which is lossy and compressed and thus, prone to artifacts.

**Justified light**
Light that appears to come from a logical source rather than appearing like a studio flood lamp. An example would be light that appears to come from a diver's flashlight.

**Key light**
Key light highlights the form and dimension of the subject.

**Lens speed**
Maximum aperture of a lens.

**Lossy compression**
This method of file management compresses data significantly and subsequently retrieves data that is different from the original, but is close enough to be useful in some way. It is associated with artifacts in compression.

**Lossless compression**
A type of data compression that allows the exact original data to be reconstructed from the compressed data without artifacts.

**Macro photography**
A type of photography that shoots very small items full frame. Some cameras have a position on the dial that is illustrated with a small flower for this mode.

**Manual mode**
"M" on a camera, indicates that the user must select both shutter and aperture values.

**Matrix metering**
A method of calculating exposure that averages readings over a large area.

**Minimum focal distance**
Distance from the camera sensor to the subject at the minimum focusing distance.

**Pixel**
The smallest unit of color & brightness in an image.

**Program mode**
"P" on a camera dial indicates that the camera will automatically decide on the appropriate value for aperture and shutter speed.

**RAW**
A file which contains minimally processed data from the image sensor of a digital camera.

**Refraction**
The way light bends as it passes from one medium to another. The light changes speed and direction. Refraction is responsible for causing objects to appear larger and closer than they are in reality.

**Resolution**
Image resolution describes the detail of an image. It is often cited as the total number of pixels in the image, typically given as the number of megapixels, which can be calculated by multiplying pixel columns by pixel rows and dividing by one million.

**Sensor**
The silicon chip inside your camera that converts light into an electronic signal.

**Shutter speed**
Common term used to describe the effective length of time a shutter is open.

**Shutter priority**
Shutter priority refers to a setting on some cameras that allows the user to choose a specific shutter speed while the camera adjusts the aperture to ensure correct exposure.

**Slave strobe**
A strobe that fires when it senses an increase in light intensity, such as another strobe firing.

**Spot metering**
A method of calculating exposure that only uses one small area.

**Strobe sync speed**
The fastest speed at which a normal strobe can be used with a camera.

**Sync cord**
An electronic cable that connects your strobe to a camera.

**Sync speed**
The fastest shutter speed at which you can synchronize strobes with your camera's shutter.

**TIFF**
Acronym for Tagged Image File Format.

**TTL**
Acronym for "through the lens." A mechanism that evaluates and sets the exposure by measuring the light coming through the lens.

**Zoom lens**
A lens with a variable focal length.

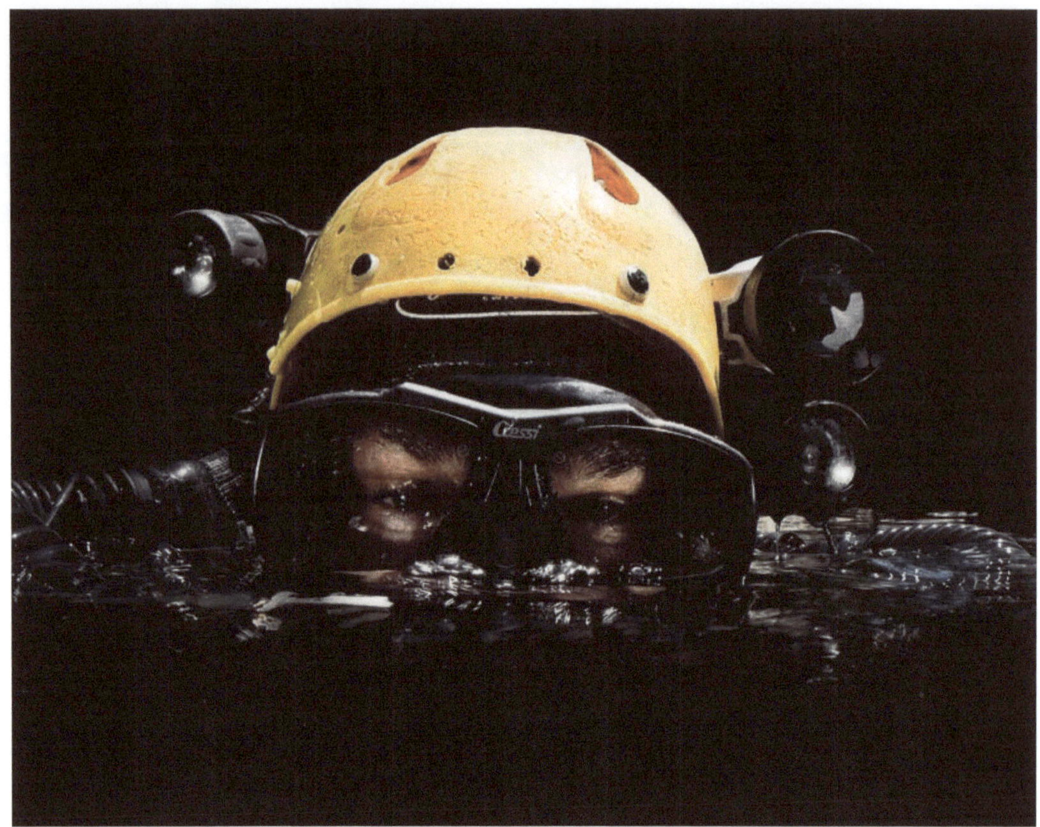

This tight shot uses dramatic lighting and an intimate close-up angle to focus the viewer on the diver's eyes.

The topside photos of this expedition are at least half the story. Your camera may be used in the housing in inclement weather or boat spray, or may be removed from the housing to catch interesting topside action.

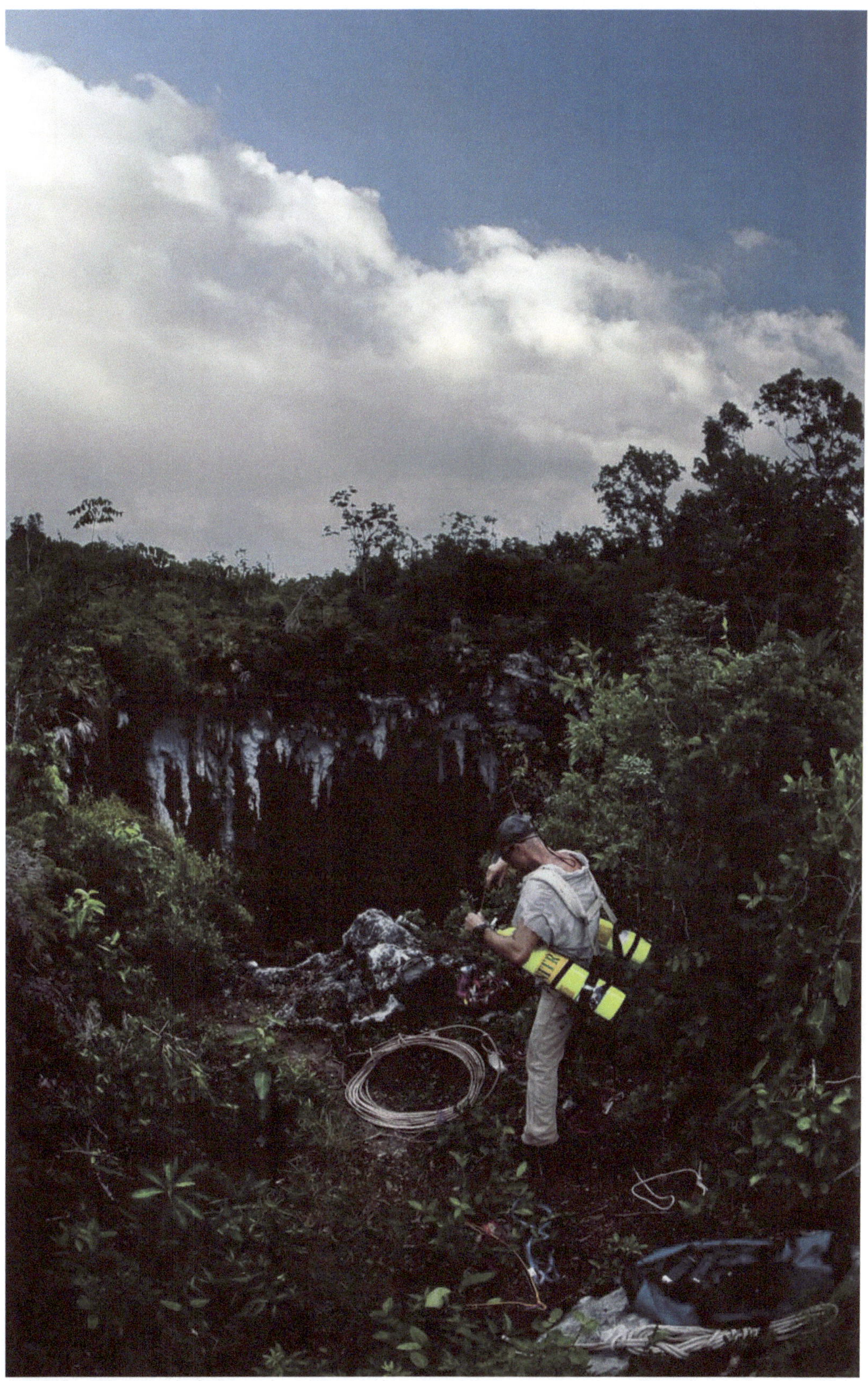

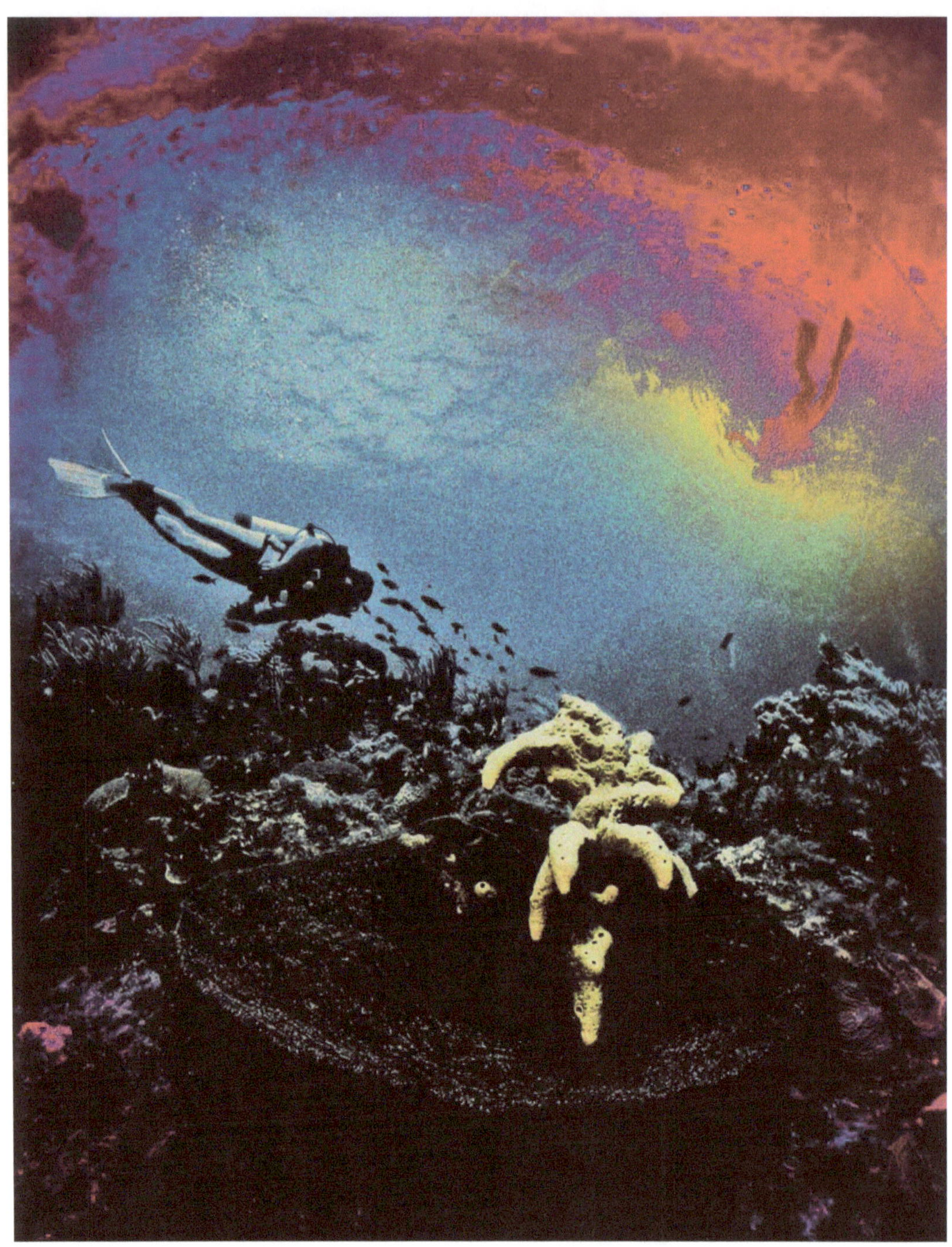

Finally... in order to distinguish yourself as a creative photographer and artist you must always think outside the box and be willing to try something fresh and new.

Experiment!

www.ingramcontent.com/pod-product-compliance
Lightning Source LLC
LaVergne TN
LVHW070509120826
845147LV00031BA/267
*9780979878923*